Explore

The Basics of Christianity,

Walking through John, Romans
and Galatians

With Guideposts by
Pastor Dan Byrne

DISCERN
PRODUCTS

Published by Discern Products
724 Parkdale Ave.
Ottawa, Ontario Canada K1Y 1J6
www.discernproducts.com

ISBN 978-1-988422-09-1

Contents

Introduction
Ready to Explore?

"People actually believe this nonsense?"

I was around 12 years old the first time I opened a Bible. I was a hurting, confused child looking for answers and unable to sleep at night. My parents had raised me to be a moral person and to respect others, but had their own issues with God, and therefore the religious environment of my family was decidedly agnostic. I suppose it could have been part of the immediate effect of their recent divorce that kept me awake at night thinking of the brevity and insecurity of life, but I seem to remember my stress coming from a different source: I was learning things in school that terrified me. At school I was taught that this world was nothing more than a product of chance; random collisions of atoms and permutations of DNA had led us to the world as is it now. And the world, is it is now, was in trouble. Air pollution, acid rain, species extinction, environmental catastrophe and global warming clouded the future. What would the world be like for me when I was my parents' age? How dare their generation hand me down such a messed up planet? Life seemed meaningless to me.

In despair one morning, I snuck into my mother's room, took her dusty Bible off the bottom shelf and scurried back to my room. "Millions of people have found comfort and meaning in the Bible," I told myself. I spent the rest of the day in my bed reading, hoping God would meet me through its pages.

I started reading as I would any other book – at the beginning. What I found was a confusing array of strange stories that seemed utterly disconnected to any of my questions. Men from dust, talking snakes, global floods, polygamy, plagues – the world I was exploring seemed more messed up than my own. Nevertheless, the stories were interesting enough to keep me reading. I read through Genesis

1

and Exodus before lunch, thinking I was doing pretty well – then I hit Leviticus. There I found confusing and, quite honestly, offensive laws that made absolutely no sense to me. But Leviticus was a breeze compared to the next book: Numbers. Numbers, as you might guess, contains large sections of nothing more than numbers. Numbers numbering people I didn't know, never heard of, and didn't care to know. The thought going through my head as I threw the Bible down in disgust and disappointment still echoes in my mind: "People actually believe this nonsense?" I snuck the Bible back into my mother's room, and didn't pick it up again for years.

Twenty-five years later, I have become one of those people who has found meaning in the pages of Scripture. I wish I could go back in time and talk to my twelve-year-old self and encourage him that his search for answers was not misplaced. I wish I could help him by simply directing him to a different starting point. The way he was trying to read the Bible was like trying to study calculus before learning how to count. I wish I could be there to guide him as he explored the Bible, so that he'd first find the answers to the questions of his soul before moving on to the advanced calculus.

While I can't go back in time, the book you are holding in your hands is my attempt to help others attempting the same exploration. I've tried to get out of the way as much as possible, for it is not in my words that you will find your answers, but in the words of Scripture itself. In this volume you will encounter God through four books of the Bible: the Gospel of John, the letters to the Roman and the Galatian churches, and the book of Psalms. These books will introduce you to Jesus Christ and contain the basic teachings of the Christian faith. I am firmly convinced that if you approach the Bible with an open heart and mind, you too will find the answers to the questions of your soul. Are you ready to explore?

How to Use This Guide

- Read with friends. You will get the most out of this guide if you set up a time once or twice a week to get together with friends and discuss what you are reading. There are a couple of reasons for this. First, reading with others will keep you motivated to press on in your exploration when life gets busy. Second, spirituality is best formed in community. You will find great benefit in wrestling through the discussion questions with other explorers. If you have a Christian friend, I'm sure they will be very happy to read with you.

- Read with an open mind. No one can force you to believe and I wouldn't dare try. But I do ask that you read with an open mind toward what you are reading. Consider the claims of Scripture for what they are. Give the Bible a fair shot.

- This book is marked with guideposts to help you address the key questions of Who is Jesus, What is the good news and What is Christian freedom. Read and ponder the marked sections before going to the commentary and questions. This procedure is designed so that God's Word speaks directly to you.

- Many excellent English translations of the Bible exist. They differ from one another for good reason; some attempt to be more faithful to the form of the underlying Greek, while others attempt to convey the meaning in ways that a modern audience will understand more clearly. In my personal study, I use many English translations, and I suggest that you do the same. This book uses three popular Bible translations (NASB, ESV and NTL) to give you a sense of the different versions and to meet the copyright restrictions placed by the owners.

Who is Jesus?
The Gospel of John

It all starts and ends with Jesus. Who is He? What made Him special? Is He God? What does it matter if He was or wasn't? These are questions that need to be answered. Thankfully, John was there, a friend and follower of Jesus. As one of the original twelve apostles, John was an eyewitness to the things Jesus said and did. He came to believe that Jesus was no ordinary man and devoted the rest of his life telling Jesus' story to everyone who would listen. In his last years, the Holy Spirit led John to record his memories of Jesus for future generations.

John was not interested in merely sharing interesting stories about Jesus with us. John had a clear purpose for writing. He writes near the end of his book that "these are written so that you may believe that Jesus is the Christ, the Son of God, and that by believing you may have life in his name." John did not record every word that Jesus said or miracle that He performed, but only those that would best demonstrate to you that Jesus is indeed who He said He was.

As you read, ask yourself: what do you think? Is John convincing?

☗ Guidepost 1
Jesus is the Word of God Among Us

1 In the beginning was the Word, and the Word was with God, and the Word was God. ² He was in the beginning with God. ³ All things were made through him, and without him was not any thing made that was made. ⁴ In him was life, and the life was the light of men. ⁵ The light shines in the darkness, and the darkness has not overcome it.

⁶ There came a man sent from God, whose name was John[a]; ⁷ He came as a witness, to bear witness about the light, that all might believe through him. ⁸ He was not the light, but came to bear witness about the light.

⁹ The true light, which gives light to everyone, was coming into the world. ¹⁰ He was in the world, and the world was made through him, yet the world did not know him. ¹¹ He came to his own, and his own people did not receive him. ¹² But to all who did receive him, who believed in his name, he gave the right to become children of God, ¹³ who were born, not of blood nor of the will of the flesh nor of the will of man, but of God.

¹⁴ And the Word became flesh and dwelt among us, and we have seen his glory, glory as of the only Son from the Father, full of grace and truth. ¹⁵ (John bore witness about him, and cried out, "This was he of whom I said, 'He who comes after me ranks before me, because he was before me.'") ¹⁶ For from his fullness we have all received, grace upon grace. ¹⁷ For the law was given through Moses; grace and truth came through Jesus Christ. ¹⁸ No one has ever seen God; the only God, who is at the Father's side, he has made him known.

---

[a] *John:* Not the author of the book but a different John, often referred to as "John the Baptist" or "John the Baptizer". This John, born a few months before Jesus, had a special mission from God to introduce Jesus to the world and to prepare people for Him

---

✝ Discussion 1
What does this guidepost teach about Jesus?

While theologians have struggled for centuries to understand Jesus' unique relationship with God, John uses two simple but profound analogies to introduce us to this amazing man that he hopes will pique our curiosity and motivate us to explore further.

First, Jesus is called the Word of God. As God's Word, Jesus existed both with and as God: divine in Himself yet distinct from the Father. How did God communicate His Word to us? By sending Him to us as one of us, the Word become flesh.

Second, Jesus is called the only Son of God. What does John mean by this? Reading closely, we see that John is setting Jesus apart as unique among men and women. Every other person has the opportunity to become a child of God as they come to Him by faith. They are, in a sense, adopted into God's family. Jesus, on the other hand, has no need to be adopted into God's family as He alone shares the Father's divine nature.

How can John make such extraordinary claims about Jesus: that a simple Middle-Eastern man like himself came from God and in fact was God? You'll have to read more to find out.

- *John clearly presents Jesus as the divine Son of God. Are you skeptical of John's claim? What is your impression of Jesus right now, as you begin this study?*
- *What does John say about the reception Jesus received when he lived among us? What response is John hoping the reader will have toward Jesus?*
- *What would it take to convince you that Jesus is who John claims He is? Will you commit to reading the rest of John's book with an open mind about Jesus?*

---

¹⁹ This is the testimony of John, when the Jews sent to him priests and Levites[b] from Jerusalem to ask him, "Who are you?" ²⁰ And he confessed and did not deny, but confessed, "I am not the Christ.[c]" ²¹ They asked him, "What then? Are you Elijah?" And he said, "I am not." "Are you the Prophet?" And he answered, "No." ²² Then they said to him, "Who are you, so that we may give an answer to those who sent us? What do you say about yourself?" ²³ He said, "I am A VOICE OF ONE CRYING IN THE WILDERNESS, 'MAKE STRAIGHT THE WAY OF THE LORD,' as Isaiah the prophet said."

²⁴ Now they had been sent from the Pharisees.[d] ²⁵ They asked him, and said to him, "Why then are you baptizing[e], if you are not the Christ, nor Elijah, nor the Prophet?" ²⁶ John answered them saying, "I baptize in water, *but* among you stands One whom you do not know. ²⁷ *It is* He who comes after me, the thong of whose sandal I am not worthy to untie." ²⁸ These things took place in Bethany beyond the Jordan, where John was baptizing.

²⁹ The next day he saw Jesus coming to him and said, "Behold, the Lamb of God[f], who takes away the sin of the world! ³⁰ This is He on

---

[b] *Priests and Levites:* Religious leaders who oversaw worship at the Temple in Jerusalem.

[c] *The Christ:* Literally, "The Anointed One". The Jewish people had been waiting for centuries for God to send them a king who would restore their kingdom and bring in a new era of peace.

[d] *Pharisees:* Members of a very strict branch of Judaism that stressed obedience to the Law God had given to the nation of Israel through a man named Moses.

[e] *Baptizing:* A ceremony of initiation in which the initiate is immersed in water, signifying death and rebirth.

[f] *Lamb of God:* The Jewish religion of Jesus' day was centered around the Temple, in which the priests and Levites would receive animal sacrifices on behalf of the people. The idea was that sin - the breaking of God's law – is such a serious offense against God that the penalty for committing sin is nothing short of death. Yet God mercifully set up a system in which the sin of the people could be atoned for through the death of an animal substitute. Clearly, this is a very foreboding thing for John to call Jesus.

behalf of whom I said, 'After me comes a Man who has a higher rank than I, for He existed before me.' [31] I did not recognize Him, but so that He might be manifested to Israel, I came baptizing in water." [32] John testified saying, "I have seen the Spirit descending as a dove out of heaven, and He remained upon Him. [33] I did not recognize Him, but He who sent me to baptize in water said to me, 'He upon whom you see the Spirit descending and remaining upon Him, this is the One who baptizes in the Holy Spirit.' [34] I myself have seen, and have testified that this is the Son of God."

[35] Again the next day John was standing with two of his disciples, [36] and he looked at Jesus as He walked, and said, "Behold, the Lamb of God!" [37] The two disciples heard him speak, and they followed Jesus. [38] And Jesus turned and saw them following, and said to them, "What do you seek?" They said to Him, "Rabbi (which translated means Teacher), where are You staying?" [39] He said to them, "Come, and you will see." So they came and saw where He was staying; and they stayed with Him that day, for it was about the tenth hour. [40] One of the two who heard John *speak* and followed Him, was Andrew, Simon Peter's brother. [41] He found first his own brother Simon and said to him, "We have found the Messiah" (which translated means Christ). [42] He brought him to Jesus. Jesus looked at him and said, "You are Simon the son of John; you shall be called Cephas" (which is translated Peter).

[43] The next day He purposed to go into Galilee, and He found Philip. And Jesus said to him, "Follow Me." [44] Now Philip was from Bethsaida, of the city of Andrew and Peter. [45] Philip found Nathanael and said to him, "We have found Him of whom Moses in the Law and *also* the Prophets wrote—Jesus of Nazareth, the son of Joseph." [46] Nathanael said to him, "Can any good thing come out of Nazareth?" Philip said to him, "Come and see." [47] Jesus saw Nathanael coming to Him, and said of him, "Behold, an Israelite indeed, in whom there is no deceit!" [48] Nathanael said to Him, "How do You know me?" Jesus answered and said to him, "Before Philip called you, when you were under the fig tree, I saw you." [49] Nathanael

answered Him, "Rabbi, You are the Son of God; You are the King of Israel." ⁵⁰ Jesus answered and said to him, "Because I said to you that I saw you under the fig tree, do you believe? You will see greater things than these." ⁵¹ And He said to him, "Truly, truly, I say to you, you will see the heavens opened and the angels of God ascending and descending on the Son of Man*ᵍ*."

2 On the third day there was a wedding in Cana of Galilee, and the mother of Jesus was there; ² and both Jesus and His disciples were invited to the wedding. ³ When the wine ran out, the mother of Jesus said to Him, "They have no wine." ⁴ And Jesus said to her, "Woman, what does that have to do with us? My hour has not yet come." ⁵ His mother said to the servants, "Whatever He says to you, do it." ⁶ Now there were six stone waterpots set there for the Jewish custom of purification, containing twenty or thirty gallons each. ⁷ Jesus said to them, "Fill the waterpots with water." So they filled them up to the brim.⁸ And He said to them, "Draw *some* out now and take it to the headwaiter." So they took it *to him*. ⁹ When the headwaiter tasted the water which had become wine, and did not know where it came from (but the servants who had drawn the water knew), the headwaiter called the bridegroom, ¹⁰ and said to him, "Every man serves the good wine first, and when *the people* have drunk freely, *then he serves* the poorer *wine; but* you have kept the good wine until now." ¹¹ This beginning of *His* signs Jesus did in Cana of Galilee, and manifested His glory, and His disciples believed in Him.

¹² After this He went down to Capernaum, He and His mother and *His* brothers and His disciples; and they stayed there a few days.

ᵍ *Son of Man*: Jesus' favorite term by which He called himself. The prophet Daniel described the coming king in this way: "Behold, with the clouds of heaven there came one like a son of man, and he came to the Ancient of Days and was presented before him. And to him was given dominion and glory and a kingdom, that all peoples, nations, and languages should serve him; his dominion is an everlasting dominion, which shall not pass away, and his kingdom one that shall not be destroyed."

13 The Passover[h] of the Jews was near, and Jesus went up to Jerusalem. 14 And He found in the temple those who were selling oxen and sheep and doves, and the money changers seated *at their tables*. 15 And He made a scourge of cords, and drove *them* all out of the temple, with the sheep and the oxen; and He poured out the coins of the money changers and overturned their tables; 16 and to those who were selling the doves He said, "Take these things away; stop making My Father's house a place of business." 17 His disciples remembered that it was written, "ZEAL FOR YOUR HOUSE WILL CONSUME ME." 18 The Jews then said to Him, "What sign do You show us as your authority for doing these things?" 19 Jesus answered them, "Destroy this temple, and in three days I will raise it up." 20 The Jews then said, "It took forty-six years to build this temple, and will You raise it up in three days?" 21 But He was speaking of the temple of His body. 22 So when He was raised from the dead, His disciples remembered that He said this; and they believed the Scripture and the word which Jesus had spoken.

23 Now when He was in Jerusalem at the Passover, during the feast, many believed in His name, observing His signs which He was doing. 24 But Jesus, on His part, wa s not entrusting Himself to them, for He knew all men, 25 and because He did not need anyone to testify concerning man, for He Himself knew what was in man.

☞ Guidepost 2
Jesus Came to Save Not to Condemn Us

3 Now there was a man of the Pharisees named Nicodemus, a ruler of the Jews. 2 This man came to Jesus by night and said to him, "Rabbi, we know that you are a teacher come from God, for no one can do these signs that you do unless God is with him." 3 Jesus

---

h *Jewish Passover:* A religious festival, still celebrated today, in which the Jewish people remember how God delivered their people from slavery in Egypt many thousands of years ago. The festival is called "Passover" because on the night of their deliverance God instructed every family to kill a lamb and cover the top of the door to their house with its blood. When the angel of death

answered him, "Truly, truly, I say to you, unless one is born again he cannot see the kingdom of God." [4] Nicodemus said to him, "How can a man be born when he is old? Can he enter a second time into his mother's womb and be born?" [5] Jesus answered, "Truly, truly, I say to you, unless one is born of water and the Spirit, he cannot enter the kingdom of God. [6] That which is born of the flesh is flesh, and that which is born of the Spirit is spirit. [7] Do not marvel that I said to you, 'You must be born again.' [8] The wind blows where it wishes, and you hear its sound, but you do not know where it comes from or where it goes. So it is with everyone who is born of the Spirit."

[9] Nicodemus said to him, "How can these things be?" [10] Jesus answered him, "Are you the teacher of Israel and yet you do not understand these things? [11] Truly, truly, I say to you, we speak of what we know, and bear witness to what we have seen, but you do not receive our testimony. [12] If I have told you earthly things and you do not believe, how can you believe if I tell you heavenly things? [13] No one has ascended into heaven except he who descended from heaven, the Son of Man. [14] And as Moses lifted up the serpent in the wilderness[i], so must the Son of Man be lifted up, [15] that whoever believes in him may have eternal life.

[16] "For God so loved the world, that he gave his only Son, that whoever believes in him should not perish but have eternal life. [17] For God did not send his Son into the world to condemn the world, but in order that the world might be saved through him. [18] Whoever believes in him is not condemned, but whoever does not believe is condemned already, because he has not believed in the name of the only Son of God. [19] And this is the judgment: the light has come into the world, and people loved the darkness rather than the light because their works were evil. [20] For everyone who does wicked things hates the light and does not come to the light, lest his works should be exposed. [21] But whoever does what is true comes to the light, so that it may be clearly seen that his works have been carried out in God."

---

[i] *as Moses lifted up the serpent in the wilderness:* Jesus is referring to a time in Israel's history when God afflicted the people with a plague of snake bites. To be saved, one needed to set their eyes upon a bronze serpent that Moses had set up on a pole. Jesus said that in the same way he would be lifted up before all men, and that we should look to Him and be saved.

📍 Discussion 2

What does this guidepost teach about Jesus?

Some people feel a sense of guilt before God that keeps them from exploring what the Bible has to say about Jesus. At times, religious people make things worse by heaping condemnation and judgement upon others, driving them away. Yet Jesus paints a completely different picture. First, Jesus tells us that God's acceptance of us is not based on our deeds but in His love. God loved us even while we were still guilty before Him. Second, Jesus reveals that God sent Him on a rescue mission. We all stood condemned before God in our sin, yet Jesus was sent to save us. When we trust in Jesus, not only are we set free from condemnation, but God's Spirit also causes us to be "re-born" to a new life, a life that begins now and extends into eternity.

- *What does it mean to be "born-again" according to this entire passage?*
- *How does guilt keep some people from coming to God? Have you ever experienced this?*
- *Does God love us because of what we do or in spite of what we do? What's the difference?*

---

²² After these things Jesus and His disciples came into the land of Judea, and there He was spending time with them and baptizing. ²³ John also was baptizing in Aenon near Salim, because there was much water there; and *people* were coming and were being baptized— ²⁴ for John had not yet been thrown into prison.

²⁵ Therefore there arose a discussion on the part of John's disciples with a Jew about purification. ²⁶ And they came to John and said to him, "Rabbi, He who was with you beyond the Jordan, to whom you have testified, behold, He is baptizing and all are coming to Him." ²⁷ John answered and said, "A man can receive nothing unless it has been given him from heaven. ²⁸ You yourselves are my witnesses that I said, 'I am not the Christ,' but, 'I have been sent ahead of Him.' ²⁹ He who has the bride is the bridegroom; but the friend of the

bridegroom, who stands and hears him, rejoices greatly because of the bridegroom's voice. So this joy of mine has been made full. [30]He must increase, but I must decrease.

[31] "He who comes from above is above all, he who is of the earth is from the earth and speaks of the earth. He who comes from heaven is above all. [32] What He has seen and heard, of that He testifies; and no one receives His testimony. [33] He who has received His testimony has set his seal to *this*, that God is true. [34] For He whom God has sent speaks the words of God; for He gives the Spirit without measure. [35] The Father loves the Son and has given all things into His hand. [36] He who believes in the Son has eternal life; but he who does not obey the Son will not see life, but the wrath of God abides on him."

4 Therefore when the Lord knew that the Pharisees had heard that Jesus was making and baptizing more disciples than John [2] (although Jesus Himself was not baptizing, but His disciples were), [3] He left Judea and went away again into Galilee. [4] And He had to pass through Samaria. [5] So He came to a city of Samaria called Sychar, near the parcel of ground that Jacob gave to his son Joseph; [6] and Jacob's well was there. So Jesus, being wearied from His journey, was sitting thus by the well. It was about the sixth hour.

[7] There came a woman of Samaria to draw water. Jesus said to her, "Give Me a drink." [8] For His disciples had gone away into the city to buy food. [9] Therefore the Samaritan[j] woman said to Him, said to Him, "How is it that You, being a Jew, ask me for a drink since I am a Samaritan woman?" (For Jews have no dealings with Samaritans.) [10] Jesus answered and said to her, "If you knew the gift of God, and who it is who says to you, 'Give Me a drink,' you would have asked Him, and He would have given you living water." [11] She said to Him, "Sir, You have nothing to draw with and the well is deep; where then

---

[j] *Samaritans.* The Samaritans were a people group of mixed ethnicity, the result of intermarriage between Jews and non-Jews. They were despised by the Jewish people of the day.

do You get that living water? [12] You are not greater than our father Jacob, are You, who gave us the well, and drank of it himself and his sons and his cattle?" [13] Jesus answered and said to her, "Everyone who drinks of this water will thirst again; [14] but whoever drinks of the water that I will give him shall never thirst; but the water that I will give him will become in him a well of water springing up to eternal life."

[15] The woman said to Him, "Sir, give me this water, so I will not be thirsty nor come all the way here to draw." [16] He said to her, "Go, call your husband and come here." [17] The woman answered and said, "I have no husband." Jesus said to her, "You have correctly said, 'I have no husband'; [18] for you have had five husbands, and the one whom you now have is not your husband; this you have said truly." [19] The woman said to Him, "Sir, I perceive that You are a prophet. [20] Our fathers worshiped in this mountain[k], and you *people* say that in Jerusalem is the place where men ought to worship." [21] Jesus said to her, "Woman, believe Me, an hour is coming when neither in this mountain nor in Jerusalem will you worship the Father. [22] You worship what you do not know; we worship what we know, for salvation is from the Jews. [23] But an hour is coming, and now is, when the true worshipers will worship the Father in spirit and truth; for such people the Father seeks to be His worshipers. [24] God is spirit, and those who worship Him must worship in spirit and truth." [25] The woman said to Him, "I know that Messiah is coming (He who is called Christ); when that One comes, He will declare all things to us." [26] Jesus said to her, "I who speak to you am *He.*"

[27] At this point His disciples came, and they were amazed that He had been speaking with a woman, yet no one said, "What do You seek?" or, "Why do You speak with her?" [28] So the woman left her

---

[k] *Our fathers worshiped in this mountain*: Notice how quickly the women changes the subject! We often grow uncomfortable when our own sin is pointed out to us; yet later, she would tell the townspeople that this is the very reason she believed in Jesus, "He told me all that I ever did."

waterpot, and went into the city and said to the men, **29** "Come, see a man who told me all the things that I *have* done; this is not the Christ, is it?" **30** They went out of the city, and were coming to Him.

31 Meanwhile the disciples were urging Him, saying, "Rabbi, eat." **32** But He said to them, "I have food to eat that you do not know about." **33** So the disciples were saying to one another, "No one brought Him *anything* to eat, did he?" **34** Jesus said to them, "My food is to do the will of Him who sent Me and to accomplish His work. **35** Do you not say, 'There are yet four months, and *then* comes the harvest'? Behold, I say to you, lift up your eyes and look on the fields, that they are white for harvest. **36** Already he who reaps is receiving wages and is gathering fruit for life eternal; so that he who sows and he who reaps may rejoice together. **37** For in this *case* the saying is true, 'One sows and another reaps.' **38** I sent you to reap that for which you have not labored; others have labored and you have entered into their labor."

39 From that city many of the Samaritans believed in Him because of the word of the woman who testified, "He told me all the things that I *have* done." **40** So when the Samaritans came to Jesus, they were asking Him to stay with them; and He stayed there two days. **41** Many more believed because of His word; **42** and they were saying to the woman, "It is no longer because of what you said that we believe, for we have heard for ourselves and know that this One is indeed the Savior of the world."

43 After the two days He went forth from there into Galilee. **44** For Jesus Himself testified that a prophet has no honor in his own country. **45** So when He came to Galilee, the Galileans received Him, having seen all the things that He did in Jerusalem at the feast; for they themselves also went to the feast.

46 Therefore He came again to Cana of Galilee where He had made the water wine. And there was a royal official whose son was sick at Capernaum. **47** When he heard that Jesus had come out of Judea into Galilee, he went to Him and was imploring *Him* to come down and heal his son; for he was at the point of death. **48** So Jesus said to him,

"Unless you *people* see signs and wonders, you *simply* will not believe." **49** The royal official said to Him, "Sir, come down before my child dies."**50** Jesus said to him, "Go; your son lives." The man believed the word that Jesus spoke to him and started off. **51** As he was now going down, *his* slaves met him, saying that his son was living. **52** So he inquired of them the hour when he began to get better. Then they said to him, "Yesterday at the seventh hour the fever left him." **53** So the father knew that *it was* at that hour in which Jesus said to him, "Your son lives"; and he himself believed and his whole household. **54** This is again a second sign that Jesus performed when He had come out of Judea into Galilee.

5 After these things there was a feast of the Jews, and Jesus went up to Jerusalem.

2 Now there is in Jerusalem by the sheep *gate* a pool, which is called in Hebrew Bethesda[1], having five porticoes. **3** In these lay a multitude of those who were sick, blind, lame, and withered, waiting for the moving of the waters; **4** for an angel of the Lord went down at certain seasons into the pool and stirred up the water; whoever then first, after the stirring up of the water, stepped in was made well from whatever disease with which he was afflicted. **5** A man was there who had been ill for thirty-eight years. **6** When Jesus saw him lying *there*, and knew that he had already been a long time *in that condition*, He said to him, "Do you wish to get well?" **7** The sick man answered Him, "Sir, I have no man to put me into the pool when the water is stirred up, but while I am coming, another steps down before me." **8** Jesus said to him, "Get up, pick up your pallet and walk." **9** Immediately the man became well, and picked up his pallet and *began* to walk.

Now it was the Sabbath on that day. **10** So the Jews were saying to the man who was cured, "It is the Sabbath, and it is not permissible for you to carry your pallet." **11** But he answered them, "He who made

---

[1] *Bethesda*: People believed that the pool of Bethesda had healing properties, so many had come to these waters.

me well was the one who said to me, 'Pick up your pallet and walk.'"
[12] They asked him, "Who is the man who said to you, 'Pick up *your pallet* and walk'?" [13] But the man who was healed did not know who it was, for Jesus had slipped away while there was a crowd in *that* place. [14] Afterward Jesus found him in the temple and said to him, "Behold, you have become well; do not sin anymore, so that nothing worse happens to you." [15] The man went away, and told the Jews that it was Jesus who had made him well. [16] For this reason the Jews were persecuting Jesus, because He was doing these things on the Sabbath[m]. [17] But He answered them, "My Father is working until now, and I Myself am working."

[18] For this reason therefore the Jews were seeking all the more to kill Him, because He not only was breaking the Sabbath, but also was calling God His own Father, making Himself equal with God[n].

[19] Therefore Jesus answered and was saying to them, "Truly, truly, I say to you, the Son can do nothing of Himself, unless *it is* something He sees the Father doing; for whatever the Father does, these things the Son also does in like manner. [20] For the Father loves the Son, and shows Him all things that He Himself is doing; and *the Father* will show Him greater works than these, so that you will marvel. [21] For just as the Father raises the dead and gives them life, even so the Son also gives life to whom He wishes. [22] For not even the Father judges anyone, but He has given all judgment to the Son, [23] so that all will honor the Son even as they honor the Father. He who does not honor the Son does not honor the Father who sent Him.

---

[m] *Sabbath*: Every week the Jewish people observe a day of rest and worship from Friday at sundown until Saturday at sundown. God had commanded them to do this in the Law of Moses. However, by Jesus' time religious people had made up many, many rules dictating *how* people were to observe Sabbath. Jesus challenged these man-made rules.
[n] *Making himself equal with God*: Some people argue that Jesus never claimed equality with God for Himself, yet John says that this is precisely the claim that those who heard Jesus understood that Jesus was making.

²⁴ "Truly, truly, I say to you, he who hears My word, and believes Him who sent Me, has eternal life, and does not come into judgment, but has passed out of death into life.

²⁵ Truly, truly, I say to you, an hour is coming and now is, when the dead will hear the voice of the Son of God, and those who hear will live. ²⁶ For just as the Father has life in Himself, even so He gave to the Son also to have life in Himself; ²⁷ and He gave Him authority to execute judgment, because He is *the* Son of Man. ²⁸ Do not marvel at this; for an hour is coming, in which all who are in the tombs will hear His voice, ²⁹ and will come forth; those who did the good *deeds* to a resurrection of life, those who committed the evil *deeds* to a resurrection of judgment.

³⁰ "I can do nothing on My own initiative. As I hear, I judge; and My judgment is just, because I do not seek My own will, but the will of Him who sent Me.

³¹ "If I *alone* testify about Myself, My testimony is not true°. ³² There is another who testifies of Me, and I know that the testimony which He gives about Me is true.

³³ You have sent to John, and he has testified to the truth. ³⁴ But the testimony which I receive is not from man, but I say these things so that you may be saved. ³⁵ He was the lamp that was burning and was shining and you were willing to rejoice for a while in his light.

³⁶ But the testimony which I have is greater than *the testimony of* John; for the works which the Father has given Me to accomplish— the very works that I do—testify about Me, that the Father has sent Me.

³⁷ And the Father who sent Me, He has testified of Me. You have neither heard His voice at any time nor seen His form. ³⁸ You do not

---

° *If I alone testify about Myself, My testimony is not true*: In this amazing speech by Jesus He concedes that His own testimony about himself would not hold up before others, so he introduces other witness who would testify on his behalf. John the baptizer is a human witness. The works Jesus did also testified of who He was. Moreover, the Father himself spoke from heaven, testifying of the Son. Finally, the scriptures written by Moses, which the Jews held in such high esteem, also spoke of Jesus.

have His word abiding in you, for you do not believe Him whom He sent.

39 You search the Scriptures because you think that in them you have eternal life; it is these that testify about Me; 40 and you are unwilling to come to Me so that you may have life. 41 I do not receive glory from men; 42 but I know you, that you do not have the love of God in yourselves. 43 I have come in My Father's name, and you do not receive Me; if another comes in his own name, you will receive him. 44 How can you believe, when you receive glory from one another and you do not seek the glory that is from the *one and* only God? 45 Do not think that I will accuse you before the Father; the one who accuses you is Moses, in whom you have set your hope. 46 For if you believed Moses, you would believe Me, for he wrote about Me. 47 But if you do not believe his writings, how will you believe My words?"

6 After these things Jesus went away to the other side of the Sea of Galilee (or Tiberias). 2 A large crowd followed Him, because they saw the signs which He was performing on those who were sick. 3 Then Jesus went up on the mountain, and there He sat down with His disciples. 4 Now the Passover, the feast of the Jews, was near. 5 Therefore Jesus, lifting up His eyes and seeing that a large crowd was coming to Him, said to Philip, "Where are we to buy bread, so that these may eat?" 6 This He was saying to test him, for He Himself knew what He was intending to do. 7 Philip answered Him, "Two hundred denarii worth of bread is not sufficient for them, for everyone to receive a little." 8 One of His disciples, Andrew, Simon Peter's brother, said to Him, 9 "There is a lad here who has five barley loaves and two fish, but what are these for so many people?" 10 Jesus said, "Have the people sit down." Now there was much grass in the place. So the men sat down, in number about five thousand. 11 Jesus then took the loaves, and having given thanks, He distributed to those who were seated; likewise also of the fish as much as they wanted. 12 When they were filled, He said to His disciples, "Gather up the leftover fragments so that nothing will be lost." ¹³ So they gathered them up, and filled twelve baskets with fragments from the five barley loaves which were left over by those who had eaten.¹⁴ Therefore when the people saw the sign which He had performed, they said, "This is truly the Prophet who is to come into the world."

¹⁵ So Jesus, perceiving that they were intending to come and take Him by force to make Him king, withdrew again to the mountain by Himself alone.

¹⁶ Now when evening came, His disciples went down to the sea, ¹⁷ and after getting into a boat, they *started to* cross the sea to Capernaum. It had already become dark, and Jesus had not yet come to them. ¹⁸ The sea *began* to be stirred up because a strong wind was blowing. ¹⁹ Then, when they had rowed about three or four miles, they saw Jesus walking on the sea and drawing near to the boat; and they were frightened. ²⁰ But He said to them, "It is I; do not be afraid." ²¹ So they were willing to receive Him into the boat, and immediately the boat was at the land to which they were going.

⚑ Guidepost 3
Jesus is the Bread of Life
("I Am" Statement 1)

²² On the next day the crowd that remained on the other side of the sea saw that there had been only one boat there, and that Jesus had not entered the boat with his disciples, but that his disciples had gone away alone. ²³ Other boats from Tiberias came near the place where they had eaten the bread after the Lord had given thanks. ²⁴ So when the crowd saw that Jesus was not there, nor his disciples, they themselves got into the boats and went to Capernaum, seeking Jesus.

²⁵ When they found him on the other side of the sea, they said to him, "Rabbi, when did you come here?" ²⁶ Jesus answered them, "Truly, truly, I say to you, you are seeking me, not because you saw

signs, but because you ate your fill of the loaves. [27] Do not work for the food that perishes, but for the food that endures to eternal life, which the Son of Man will give to you. For on him God the Father has set his seal." [28] Then they said to him, "What must we do, to be doing the works of God?" [29] Jesus answered them, "This is the work of God, that you believe in him whom he has sent." [30] So they said to him, "Then what sign do you do, that we may see and believe you? What work do you perform? [31] Our fathers ate the manna in the wilderness; as it is written, 'He gave them bread from heaven to eat.'" [32] Jesus then said to them, "Truly, truly, I say to you, it was not Moses who gave you the bread from heaven, but my Father gives you the true bread from heaven. [33] For the bread of God is he who comes down from heaven and gives life to the world." [34] They said to him, "Sir, give us this bread always."

[35] Jesus said to them, "I am the bread of life; whoever comes to me shall not hunger, and whoever believes in me shall never thirst. [36] But I said to you that you have seen me and yet do not believe. [37] All that the Father gives me will come to me, and whoever comes to me I will never cast out. [38] For I have come down from heaven, not to do my own will but the will of him who sent me. [39] And this is the will of him who sent me, that I should lose nothing of all that he has given me, but raise it up on the last day. [40] For this is the will of my Father, that everyone who looks on the Son and believes in him should have eternal life, and I will raise him up on the last day."

☞ Discussion 3

What does this guidepost teach about Jesus?

In this passage, Jesus claims, "I am the bread of life." This is the first of seven notable "I am..." statements that Jesus makes about Himself in the Book of John. Just as bread is essential for life, so Jesus offered himself as the sustainer of life to all who would come to him.

After Moses led the people out of slavery in Egypt the nation of Israel wandered in the wilderness for forty years. During that time God sustained them by providing for them a flaky bread-like substance that covered the ground each morning. The Israelites did not labor for this "bread-from-heaven"; they received it as a gift from God each day. Jesus was teaching that we cannot work to try to earn salvation from God. Instead, the "work" God requires from us is to believe in His Son whom He has sent to offer us eternal life.

This concept that we cannot work for our salvation but only must receive it is referred to in the Bible as *grace* and is foundational to understanding the Christian way of relating to God. Every other religion teaches us that we must purify ourselves before God will accept us. Christianity declares that God accepts us as we are by graciously sending His Son for us. We cannot work to try to earn God's favor - but instead must receive God's salvation as a gift. This contrast will become more pronounced as we make our way through Scripture.

- *What does it mean for Jesus to be the bread of life, and how can one find nourishment in Him?*
- *What are some ways that people attempt to earn a good standing with God?*

> • *Do you think anyone could ever work hard enough to make themselves morally acceptable to God? How would they know when they had done enough?*
>
> • *How does an understanding of grace guard us from becoming proud in our own religion or morality?*

[41] Therefore the Jews were grumbling about Him, because He said, "I am the bread that came down out of heaven." [42] They were saying, "Is not this Jesus, the son of Joseph, whose father and mother we know? How does He now say, 'I have come down out of heaven'?" [43] Jesus answered and said to them, "Do not grumble among yourselves. [44] No one can come to Me unless the Father who sent Me draws him; and I will raise him up on the last day. [45] It is written in the prophets, 'AND THEY SHALL ALL BE TAUGHT OF GOD.' Everyone who has heard and learned from the Father, comes to Me. [46] Not that anyone has seen the Father, except the One who is from God; He has seen the Father. [47] Truly, truly, I say to you, he who believes has eternal life. [48] I am the bread of life. [49] Your fathers ate the manna in the wilderness, and they died. [50] This is the bread which comes down out of heaven, so that one may eat of it and not die. [51] I am the living bread that came down out of heaven; if anyone eats of this bread[p], he will live forever; and the bread also which I will give for the life of the world is My flesh."

[52] Then the Jews *began* to argue with one another, saying, "How can this man give us *His* flesh to eat?" [53] So Jesus said to them, "Truly, truly, I say to you, unless you eat the flesh of the Son of Man and drink His blood, you have no life in yourselves. [54] He who eats My

---

[p] *If anyone eats of this bread*: Jesus is speaking metaphorically, that we must receive Him by believing in Him. However, in His next statement He alludes to the fact that He will ultimately give His own flesh – His own life – for us to be saved. There is a sense in which Jesus gave His own life to be consumed by the world.

flesh and drinks My blood[q] has eternal life, and I will raise him up on the last day. [55] For My flesh is true food, and My blood is true drink. [56] He who eats My flesh and drinks My blood abides in Me, and I in him. [57] As the living Father sent Me, and I live because of the Father, so he who eats Me, he also will live because of Me. [58] This is the bread which came down out of heaven; not as the fathers ate and died; he who eats this bread will live forever."

[59] These things He said in the synagogue as He taught in Capernaum.

[60] Therefore many of His disciples, when they heard *this* said, "This is a difficult statement; who can listen to it?" [61] But Jesus, conscious that His disciples grumbled at this, said to them, "Does this cause you to stumble? [62] *What* then if you see the Son of Man ascending to where He was before? [63] It is the Spirit who gives life; the flesh profits nothing; the words that I have spoken to you are spirit and are life. [64] But there are some of you who do not believe." For Jesus knew from the beginning who they were who did not believe, and who it was that would betray Him. [65] And He was saying, "For this reason I have said to you, that no one can come to Me unless it has been granted him from the Father."

[66] As a result of this many of His disciples withdrew and were not walking with Him anymore. [67] So Jesus said to the twelve, "You do not want to go away also, do you?" [68] Simon Peter answered Him, "Lord, to whom shall we go? You have words of eternal life. [69] We have believed and have come to know that You are the Holy One of God." [70] Jesus answered them, "Did I Myself not choose you, the twelve, and *yet* one of you is a devil?" [71] Now He meant Judas *the son* of Simon Iscariot, for he, one of the twelve, was going to betray Him.

---

[q] *Eats My flesh and drinks my blood*: Jesus is using an admittedly gruesome metaphor to point out two things. First, He will literally give his whole life, flesh and blood, for us to be saved. Second, we must receive Him and the sacrifice that He has made. Christians use the same metaphor when we celebrate the Lord's Supper. We eat bread to remember that Jesus willingly gave His life for us, and drink a cup of red wine remembering that His blood was poured out for us.

7 After these things Jesus was walking in Galilee, for He was unwilling to walk in Judea because the Jews were seeking to kill Him. ² Now the feast of the Jews, the Feast of Booths, was near. ³ Therefore His brothers said to Him, "Leave here and go into Judea, so that Your disciples also may see Your works which You are doing. ⁴ For no one does anything in secret when he himself seeks to be *known* publicly. If You do these things, show Yourself to the world." ⁵ For not even His brothers were believing in Him. ⁶ So Jesus said to them, "My time is not yet here, but your time is always opportune. ⁷ The world cannot hate you, but it hates Me because I testify of it, that its deeds are evil. ⁸ Go up to the feast yourselves; I do not go up to this feast because My time has not yet fully come." ⁹ Having said these things to them, He stayed in Galilee.

¹⁰ But when His brothers had gone up to the feast, then He Himself also went up, not publicly, but as if, in secret. ¹¹ So the Jews were seeking Him at the feast and were saying, "Where is He?" ¹² There was much grumbling among the crowds concerning Him; some were saying, "He is a good manʳ"; others were saying, "No, on the contrary, He leads the people astray." ¹³ Yet no one was speaking openly of Him for fear of the Jews.

¹⁴ But when it was now the midst of the feast Jesus went up into the temple, and *began to* teach. ¹⁵ The Jews then were astonished, saying, "How has this man become learned, having never been educated?" ¹⁶ So Jesus answered them and said, "My teaching is not Mine, but His who sent Me. ¹⁷ If anyone is willing to do His will, he will know of the teaching, whether it is of God or *whether* I speak from Myself. ¹⁸ He who speaks from himself seeks his own glory; but He who is seeking the glory of the One who sent Him, He is true, and there is no unrighteousness in Him.

ʳ *He is a good man*: Even today, many believe Jesus to be nothing more than a good man. Yet a man who made the claims Jesus made about Himself either was speaking the truth, in which case He would be much more than a good man, or lying and leading the people astray

19 "Did not Moses give you the Law, and *yet* none of you carries out the Law? Why do you seek to kill Me?" 20 The crowd answered, "You have a demon! Who seeks to kill You?" 21 Jesus answered them, "I did one deed, and you all marvel. 22 For this reason Moses has given you circumcision* (not because it is from Moses, but from the fathers), and on *the* Sabbath you circumcise a man. 23 If a man receives circumcision on *the* Sabbath so that the Law of Moses will not be broken, are you angry with Me because I made an entire man well on *the* Sabbath? 24 Do not judge according to appearance, but judge with righteous judgment."

25 So some of the people of Jerusalem were saying, "Is this not the man whom they are seeking to kill? 26 Look, He is speaking publicly, and they are saying nothing to Him. The rulers do not really know that this is the Christ, do they? 27 However, we know where this man is from; but whenever the Christ may come, no one knows where He is from." 28 Then Jesus cried out in the temple, teaching and saying, "You both know Me and know where I am from; and I have not come of Myself, but He who sent Me is true, whom you do not know. 29 I know Him, because I am from Him, and He sent Me." 30 So they were seeking to seize Him; and no man laid his hand on Him, because His hour had not yet come. 31 But many of the crowd believed in Him; and they were saying, "When the Christ comes, He will not perform more signs than those which this man has, will He?"

32 The Pharisees heard the crowd muttering these things about Him, and the chief priests and the Pharisees sent officers to seize Him. 33 Therefore Jesus said, "For a little while longer I am with you, then I go to Him who sent Me. 34 You will seek Me, and will not find Me; and where I am, you cannot come." 35 The Jews then said to one another, "Where does this man intend to go that we will not find Him? He is not intending to go to the Dispersion among the Greeks, and teach the Greeks, is He? 36 What is this statement that He said,

---

* *Circumcision*: As an outward sign of the Jews devotion to God, the law of Moses requires every male to be circumcised.

'You will seek Me, and will not find Me; and where I am, you cannot come'?"

🪧 Guidepost 4
Jesus is the Light of the World
("I Am" Statement 2)

37 On the last day of the feast, the great day, Jesus stood up and cried out, "If anyone thirsts, let him come to me and drink. 38 Whoever believes in me, as the Scripture has said, 'Out of his heart will flow rivers of living water.'" 39 Now this he said about the Spirit, whom those who believed in him were to receive, for as yet the Spirit had not been given, because Jesus was not yet glorified.

40 When they heard these words, some of the people said, "This really is the Prophet." 41 Others said, "This is the Christ." But some said, "Is the Christ to come from Galilee? 42 Has not the Scripture said that the Christ comes from the offspring of David, and comes from Bethlehem[t], the village where David was?" 43 So there was a division among the people over him. 44 Some of them wanted to arrest him, but no one laid hands on him.

45 The officers then came to the chief priests and Pharisees, who said to them, "Why did you not bring him?" 46 The officers answered, "No one ever spoke like this man!" 47 The Pharisees answered them, "Have you also been deceived? 48 Have any of the authorities or the Pharisees believed in him? 49 But this crowd that does not know the law is accursed." 50 Nicodemus, who had gone to him before, and who was one of them, said to them, 51 "Does our law judge a man

---

[t] *David, and from Bethlehem:* David was the greatest of the kings of Israel. God promised David that his kingdom would endure forever. The Jews of Jesus' time were looking for the rise of a new king who would fulfill this promise. It was foretold that this Messiah would come from Bethlehem. These people were not aware that Jesus was born in Bethlehem.

without first giving him a hearing and learning what he does?" [52] They replied, "Are you from Galilee too? Search and see that no prophet arises from Galilee."

[53] {They went each to his own house,

8 but Jesus went to the Mount of Olives. [2] Early in the morning he came again to the temple. All the people came to him, and he sat down and taught them. [3] The scribes and the Pharisees brought a woman who had been caught in adultery, and placing her in the midst [4] they said to him, "Teacher, this woman has been caught in the act of adultery. [5] Now in the Law, Moses commanded us to stone such women. So what do you say?" [6] This they said to test him, that they might have some charge to bring against him. Jesus bent down and wrote with his finger on the ground. [7] And as they continued to ask him, he stood up and said to them, "Let him who is without sin among you be the first to throw a stone at her." [8] And once more he bent down and wrote on the ground. [9] But when they heard it, they went away one by one, beginning with the older ones, and Jesus was left alone with the woman standing before him. [10] Jesus stood up and said to her, "Woman, where are they? Has no one condemned you?" [11] She said, "No one, Lord." And Jesus said, "Neither do I condemn you; go, and from now on sin no more."} [u]

[12] Again Jesus spoke to them, saying, "I am the light of the world. Whoever follows me will not walk in darkness, but will have the light of life."

---

[u] The brackets indicate that this section is disputed as being authentic, for it is not found in many of the earliest manuscripts that we have discovered. Nevertheless, many believe that the episode this passage describes may have really happened, even if it was added to the Book of John later. While it is an inspiring story, no Christian beliefs are affected by its inclusion or exclusion from the Scriptures, so most Bibles include the passage while marking it as disputed for the reader.

🚩 Discussion 4
What does this guidepost teach about Jesus?

Jesus makes his second "I am" statement on the morning after the week-long Feast of the Tabernacles. Each day during this festival, while the people waved palm branches and joyfully praised God, priests would draw out water from the pool of Siloam, proclaiming, "With joy you will draw water from the wells of salvation." Every evening, four huge pillars lit up the city in celebration. These lamps were to remind the people of the Glory of the Lord that led the people of Israel as they wandered in the wilderness. All night long Jerusalem was filled with people singing and dancing under the radiant light.

On the last day of the festival, as the priests were drawing out the water, Jesus stood up and cried out, "If anyone thirsts, let him come to me and drink." These words implied to those present that He indeed was the Messiah of God who would pour out God's Spirit upon all who believed in Him. Unsurprisingly, this caused the priests to become enraged, yet it was nothing compared to what would happen the next day when He would defy them once again by sparing the adulterous woman.

Jesus' words of grace to the adulterous women echo his remarks to Nicodemus, that he had not come into the world to condemn the world, but to save us from our sins. Jesus did not excuse her sin, but told her to live a new life freed from sin. But how? In a stunning conclusion, Jesus turned to the bewildered crowd and announced that just as the Israelites once followed the guidance of light of the Glory of God, they were now to follow Him, the true Light of the World. Only by following Him as our Light are we able to overcome sin.

> - *How did Jesus' attitude toward the woman demonstrate that he is both the refreshing water of life and the light of the world that leads people out of darkness?*
> - *What is something in your life for which you currently need guidance? What would it mean for you to follow Jesus as your light?*

13 So the Pharisees said to Him, "You are testifying about Yourself; Your testimony is not true." 14 Jesus answered and said to them, "Even if I testify about Myself, My testimony is true, for I know where I came from and where I am going; but you do not know where I come from or where I am going. 15 You judge according to the flesh; I am not judging anyone. 16 But even if I do judge, My judgment is true; for I am not alone *in it*, but I and the Father who sent Me. 17 Even in your law it has been written that the testimony of two men is true. 18 I am He who testifies about Myself, and the Father who sent Me testifies about Me." 19 So they were saying to Him, "Where is Your Father?" Jesus answered, "You know neither Me nor My Father; if you knew Me, you would know My Father also." 20 These words He spoke in the treasury, as He taught in the temple; and no one seized Him, because His hour had not yet come.

21 Then He said again to them, "I go away, and you will seek Me, and will die in your sin; where I am going, you cannot come." 22 So the Jews were saying, "Surely He will not kill Himself, will He, since He says, 'Where I am going, you cannot come'?" 23 And He was saying to them, "You are from below, I am from above; you are of this world, I am not of this world. 24 Therefore I said to you that you will die in your sins; for unless you believe that I am *He*, you will die in your sins." 25 So they were saying to Him, "Who are You?" Jesus said to them, "What have I been saying to you *from* the beginning? 26 I have many things to speak and to judge concerning you, but He who sent Me is true; and the things which I heard from Him, these I speak to the world." 27 They did not realize that He had been speaking to them

about the Father. ²⁸ So Jesus said, "When you lift up the Son of Man, then you will know that I am *He*, and I do nothing on My own initiative, but I speak these things as the Father taught Me. ²⁹ And He who sent Me is with Me; He has not left Me alone, for I always do the things that are pleasing to Him." ³⁰ As He spoke these things, many came to believe in Him.

³¹ So Jesus was saying to those Jews who had believed Him, "If you continue in My word, *then* you are truly disciples of Mine; ³² and you will know the truth, and the truth will make you free." ³³ They answered Him, "We are Abraham's descendants^v and have never yet been enslaved to anyone; how is it that You say, 'You will become free'?"

³⁴ Jesus answered them, "Truly, truly, I say to you, everyone who commits sin is the slave of sin. ³⁵ The slave does not remain in the house forever; the son does remain forever. ³⁶ So if the Son makes you free, you will be free indeed. ³⁷ I know that you are Abraham's descendants; yet you seek to kill Me, because My word has no place in you. ³⁸ I speak the things which I have seen with *My* Father; therefore you also do the things which you heard from *your* father."

³⁹ They answered and said to Him, "Abraham is our father." Jesus said to them, "If you are Abraham's children, do the deeds of Abraham. ⁴⁰ But as it is, you are seeking to kill Me, a man who has told you the truth, which I heard from God; this Abraham did not do. ⁴¹ You are doing the deeds of your father." They said to Him, "We were not born of fornication; we have one Father: God." ⁴² Jesus said to them, "If God were your Father, you would love Me, for I proceeded forth and have come from God, for I have not even come on My own initiative, but He sent Me. ⁴³ Why do you not understand what I am saying? *It is* because you cannot hear My word. ⁴⁴ You are of *your* father the devil, and you want to do the desires of your father.

---

^v *Abraham's descendants*: Abraham was the most notable ancestor of the Jewish people. God had revealed to Abraham that his descendants would bring a blessing to the world. They misunderstood this promise and proudly wore it as a badge of their superiority as a people.

He was a murderer from the beginning, and does not stand in the truth because there is no truth in him. Whenever he speaks a lie, he speaks from his own *nature*, for he is a liar and the father of lies. ⁴⁵ But because I speak the truth, you do not believe Me. ⁴⁶ Which one of you convicts Me of sin? If I speak truth, why do you not believe Me? ⁴⁷ He who is of God hears the words of God; for this reason you do not hear *them*, because you are not of God."

⁴⁸ The Jews answered and said to Him, "Do we not say rightly that You are a Samaritan and have a demon?" ⁴⁹ Jesus answered, "I do not have a demon; but I honor My Father, and you dishonor Me. ⁵⁰ But I do not seek My glory; there is One who seeks and judges. ⁵¹ Truly, truly, I say to you, if anyone keeps My word he will never see death." ⁵² The Jews said to Him, "Now we know that You have a demon. Abraham died, and the prophets *also*; and You say, 'If anyone keeps My word, he will never taste of death.' ⁵³ Surely You are not greater than our father Abraham, who died? The prophets died too; whom do You make Yourself out *to be*?" ⁵⁴ Jesus answered, "If I glorify Myself, My glory is nothing; it is My Father who glorifies Me, of whom you say, 'He is our God'; ⁵⁵ and you have not come to know Him, but I know Him; and if I say that I do not know Him, I will be a liar like you, but I do know Him and keep His word. ⁵⁶ Your father Abraham rejoiced to see My day, and he saw *it* and was glad." ⁵⁷ So the Jews said to Him, "You are not yet fifty years old, and have You seen Abraham?" ⁵⁸ Jesus said to them, "Truly, truly, I say to you, before Abraham was born, I am." ⁵⁹ Therefore they picked up stones to throw at Himʷ, but Jesus hid Himself and went out of the temple.

9 As He passed by, He saw a man blind from birth. ² And His disciples asked Him, "Rabbi, who sinned, this man or his parents, that

---

ʷ *before Abraham was born, I am." Therefore they picked up stones to throw at Him*: The Jewish name for the Lord, Yahweh, literally means "I am that I am" – the self-existing One. Jesus is declaring that He is the Lord who existed before Abraham ever came to be. To the Jewish people at the Temple this was such a blasphemous claim that they sought to kill him by stoning him.

he would be born blind?" ³ Jesus answered, "*It was* neither *that* this man sinned, nor his parents; but *it was* so that the works of God might be displayed in him. ⁴ We must work the works of Him who sent Me as long as it is day; night is coming when no one can work. ⁵ While I am in the world, I am the Light of the world." ⁶ When He had said this, He spat on the ground, and made clay of the spittle, and applied the clay to his eyes,⁷ and said to him, "Go, wash in the pool of Siloam" (which is translated, Sent). So he went away and washed, and came *back* seeing. ⁸ Therefore the neighbors, and those who previously saw him as a beggar, were saying, "Is not this the one who used to sit and beg?" ⁹ Others were saying, "This is he," *still* others were saying, "No, but he is like him." He kept saying, "I am the one." ¹⁰ So they were saying to him, "How then were your eyes opened?" ¹¹ He answered, "The man who is called Jesus made clay, and anointed my eyes, and said to me, 'Go to Siloam and wash'; so I went away and washed, and I received sight." ¹² They said to him, "Where is He?" He said, "I do not know."

¹³ They brought to the Pharisees the man who was formerly blind.¹⁴ Now it was a Sabbath on the day when Jesus made the clay and opened his eyes. ¹⁵ Then the Pharisees also were asking him again how he received his sight. And he said to them, "He applied clay to my eyes, and I washed, and I see." ¹⁶ Therefore some of the Pharisees were saying, "This man is not from God, because He does not keep the Sabbath." But others were saying, "How can a man who is a sinner perform such signs?" And there was a division among them. ¹⁷ So they said to the blind man again, "What do you say about Him, since He opened your eyes?" And he said, "He is a prophet."

¹⁸ The Jews then did not believe *it* of him, that he had been blind and had received sight, until they called the parents of the very one who had received his sight, ¹⁹ and questioned them, saying, "Is this your son, who you say was born blind? Then how does he now see?" ²⁰ His parents answered them and said, "We know that this is our son, and that he was born blind; ²¹ but how he now sees, we do not know; or who opened his eyes, we do not know. Ask him; he is of age, he

will speak for himself."²² His parents said this because they were afraid of the Jews; for the Jews had already agreed that if anyone confessed Him to be Christ, he was to be put out of the synagogue. ²³ For this reason his parents said, "He is of age; ask him."

²⁴ So a second time they called the man who had been blind, and said to him, "Give glory to God; we know that this man is a sinner." ²⁵ He then answered, "Whether He is a sinner, I do not know; one thing I do know, that though I was blind, now I see." ²⁶ So they said to him, "What did He do to you? How did He open your eyes?" ²⁷ He answered them, "I told you already and you did not listen; why do you want to hear *it* again? You do not want to become His disciples too, do you?" ²⁸ They reviled him and said, "You are His disciple, but we are disciples of Moses. ²⁹ We know that God has spoken to Moses, but as for this man, we do not know where He is from." ³⁰ The man answered and said to them, "Well, here is an amazing thing, that you do not know where He is from, and *yet* He opened my eyes. ³¹ We know that God does not hear sinners; but if anyone is God-fearing and does His will, He hears him. ³² Since the beginning of time it has never been heard that anyone opened the eyes of a person born blind. ³³ If this man were not from God, He could do nothing." ³⁴ They answered him, "You were born entirely in sins, and are you teaching us?" So they put him out.

³⁵ Jesus heard that they had put him out, and finding him, He said, "Do you believe in the Son of Man?" ³⁶ He answered, "Who is He, Lord, that I may believe in Him?" ³⁷ Jesus said to him, "You have both seen Him, and He is the one who is talking with you." ³⁸ And he said, "Lord, I believe." And he worshiped Him. ³⁹ And Jesus said, "For judgment I came into this world, so that those who do not see may see, and that those who see may become blind." ⁴⁰ Those of the Pharisees who were with Him heard these things and said to Him, "We are not blind too, are we?"⁴¹ Jesus said to them, "If you were blind, you would have no sin; but since you say, 'We see,' your sin remains.

✞ Guidepost 5

Jesus is the Door and the Good Shepherd ("I Am" Statements 3 and 4)

10 "Truly, truly, I say to you, he who does not enter the sheepfold by the door but climbs in by another way, that man is a thief and a robber. [2] But he who enters by the door is the shepherd of the sheep. [3] To him the gatekeeper opens. The sheep hear his voice, and he calls his own sheep by name and leads them out. [4] When he has brought out all his own, he goes before them, and the sheep follow him, for they know his voice. [5] A stranger they will not follow, but they will flee from him, for they do not know the voice of strangers." [6] This figure of speech Jesus used with them, but they did not understand what he was saying to them.

[7] So Jesus again said to them, "Truly, truly, I say to you, I am the door of the sheep. [8] All who came before me are thieves and robbers, but the sheep did not listen to them. [9] I am the door. If anyone enters by me, he will be saved and will go in and out and find pasture. [10] The thief comes only to steal and kill and destroy. I came that they may have life and have it abundantly. [11] I am the good shepherd. The good shepherd lays down his life for the sheep. [12] He who is a hired hand and not a shepherd, who does not own the sheep, sees the wolf coming and leaves the sheep and flees, and the wolf snatches them and scatters them. [13] He flees because he is a hired hand and cares nothing for the sheep.

[14] I am the good shepherd. I know my own and my own know me, [15] just as the Father knows me and I know the Father; and I lay down my life for the sheep. [16] And I have other sheep that are not of this fold. I must bring them also, and they will listen to my voice. So there will be one flock, one shepherd. [17] For this reason the Father loves me, because I lay down my life that I may take it up again. [18] No one takes it from me, but I lay it down of my own accord. I have authority

to lay it down, and I have authority to take it up again. This charge I have received from my Father."

☝ Discussion 5
What does this guidepost teach about Jesus?

Jesus' next two "I am" statements draw from the metaphor of a sheep pen. First, Jesus compared Himself to the door that people must enter in to be saved. Jesus is not only the gate, but also the Shepherd. Many Old Testament scriptures referred to God as our Shepherd, emphasizing His protective guidance over His people. Here, however, Jesus emphasizes the shepherd's sacrificial care for his sheep, making allusion to His own upcoming death. It is very important that we understand that Jesus willingly died for us. No one took His life from Him; He lovingly laid it down to save us.

Jesus came as a Jewish person to fulfill the promises God made to the Jews, but not all of them accepted Him. Yet here, for the first time, Jesus indicates that He did not only come for the Jews, but for non-Jewish people as well, the other sheep of another fold. All who accept Him will be saved.

- *Christians often say that they hear Jesus' voice through their heart. How do you feel about this?*
- *How has Jesus been speaking to you? Through John's book? Through your life experiences?*
- *Listening to Jesus' voice means that we recognize that He our shepherd truly sent by God. How is your understanding of Jesus being formed through this study?*

---

[19] A division occurred again among the Jews because of these words.[20] Many of them were saying, "He has a demon and is insane. Why do you listen to Him?" [21] Others were saying, "These are not the

sayings of one demon-possessed. A demon cannot open the eyes of the blind, can he?"

22 At that time the Feast of the Dedication took place at Jerusalem; 23 it was winter, and Jesus was walking in the temple in the portico of Solomon. 24 The Jews then gathered around Him, and were saying to Him, "How long will You keep us in suspense? If You are the Christ, tell us plainly." 25 Jesus answered them, "I told you, and you do not believe; the works that I do in My Father's name, these testify of Me. 26 But you do not believe because you are not of My sheep. 27 My sheep hear My voice, and I know them, and they follow Me; 28 and I give eternal life to them, and they will never perish; and no one will snatch them out of My hand. 29 My Father, who has given *them* to Me, is greater than all; and no one is able to snatch *them* out of the Father's hand. 30 I and the Father are one."

31 The Jews picked up stones again to stone Him. 32 Jesus answered them, "I showed you many good works from the Father; for which of them are you stoning Me?" 33 The Jews answered Him, "For a good work we do not stone You, but for blasphemy; and because You, being a man, make Yourself out *to be* God." 34 Jesus answered them, "Has it not been written in your Law, 'I SAID, YOU ARE GODS[x]'? 35 If he called them gods, to whom the word of God came (and the Scripture cannot be broken), 36 do you say of Him, whom the Father sanctified and sent into the world, 'You are blaspheming,' because I said, 'I am the Son of God'? 37 If I do not do the works of My Father, do not believe Me; 38 but if I do them, though you do not believe Me, believe the works, so that you may know and understand that the Father is in Me, and I in the Father." 39 Therefore they were seeking again to seize Him, and He eluded their grasp.

40 And He went away again beyond the Jordan to the place where John was first baptizing, and He was staying there. 41 Many came to

---

[x] *You are gods*. Jesus is quoting Psalm 82. In this psalm, the judges who ruled over Israel are likened to gods, for their authority was granted to them by God. Jesus is making the argument that it is not blasphemy for Him to receive worship as God, for He was sent into the world to do the work of God as God's representative.

Him and were saying, "While John performed no sign, yet everything John said about this man was true." **42** Many believed in Him there.

11 Now a certain man was sick, Lazarus of Bethany, the village of Mary and her sister Martha. **2** It was the Mary who anointed the Lord with ointment, and wiped His feet with her hair, whose brother Lazarus was sick. **3** So the sisters sent *word* to Him, saying, "Lord, behold, he whom You love is sick." **4** But when Jesus heard *this*, He said, "This sickness is not to end in death, but for the glory of God, so that the Son of God may be glorified by it." **5** Now Jesus loved Martha and her sister and Lazarus. **6** So when He heard that he was sick, He then stayed two days *longer* in the place where He was. **7** Then after this He said to the disciples, "Let us go to Judea again." **8** The disciples said to Him, "Rabbi, the Jews were just now seeking to stone You, and are You going there again?" **9** Jesus answered, "Are there not twelve hours in the day? If anyone walks in the day, he does not stumble, because he sees the light of this world. **10** But if anyone walks in the night, he stumbles, because the light is not in him." **11** This He said, and after that He said to them, "Our friend Lazarus has fallen asleep; but I go, so that I may awaken him out of sleep." **12** The disciples then said to Him, "Lord, if he has fallen asleep, he will recover." **13** Now Jesus had spoken of his death, but they thought that He was speaking of literal sleep. **14** So Jesus then said to them plainly, "Lazarus is dead, **15** and I am glad for your sakes that I was not there, so that you may believe; but let us go to him." **16** Therefore Thomas, who is called Didymus, said to *his* fellow disciples, "Let us also go, so that we may die with Him."

☞ Guidepost 6

Jesus is the Resurrection and the Life
("I Am" statement 5)

17 Now when Jesus came, he found that Lazarus had already been in the tomb four days. 18 Bethany was near Jerusalem, about two miles off,19 and many of the Jews had come to Martha and Mary to console them concerning their brother. 20 So when Martha heard that Jesus was coming, she went and met him, but Mary remained seated in the house.21 Martha said to Jesus, "Lord, if you had been here, my brother would not have died. 22 But even now I know that whatever you ask from God, God will give you." 23 Jesus said to her, "Your brother will rise again."24 Martha said to him, "I know that he will rise again in the resurrection on the last day." 25 Jesus said to her, "I am the resurrection and the life. Whoever believes in me, though he die, yet shall he live, 26 and everyone who lives and believes in me shall never die. Do you believe this?" 27 She said to him, "Yes, Lord; I believe that you are the Christ, the Son of God, who is coming into the world."

28 When she had said this, she went and called her sister Mary, saying in private, "The Teacher is here and is calling for you." 29 And when she heard it, she rose quickly and went to him. 30 Now Jesus had not yet come into the village, but was still in the place where Martha had met him. 31 When the Jews who were with her in the house, consoling her, saw Mary rise quickly and go out, they followed her, supposing that she was going to the tomb to weep there. 32 Now when Mary came to where Jesus was and saw him, she fell at his feet, saying to him, "Lord, if you had been here, my brother would not have died." 33 When Jesus saw her weeping, and the Jews who had come with her also weeping, he was deeply moved in his spirit and greatly troubled. 34 And he said, "Where have you laid him?" They said to him, "Lord, come and see." 35 Jesus wept. 36 So the Jews said, "See how he loved him!" 37 But some of them said, "Could not he

who opened the eyes of the blind man also have kept this man from dying?"

[38] Then Jesus, deeply moved again, came to the tomb. It was a cave, and a stone lay against it. [39] Jesus said, "Take away the stone." Martha, the sister of the dead man, said to him, "Lord, by this time there will be an odor, for he has been dead four days." [40] Jesus said to her, "Did I not tell you that if you believed you would see the glory of God?" [41] So they took away the stone. And Jesus lifted up his eyes and said, "Father, I thank you that you have heard me. [42] I knew that you always hear me, but I said this on account of the people standing around, that they may believe that you sent me." [43] When he had said these things, he cried out with a loud voice, "Lazarus, come out." [44] The man who had died came out, his hands and feet bound with linen strips, and his face wrapped with a cloth. Jesus said to them, "Unbind him, and let him go."

☛ Discussion 6
What does this guidepost teach about Jesus?

It has been said that the only sure things in life are death and taxes. Throughout history, mankind has speculated on the question of whether or not there is life after death. The Jews of Jesus' day believed that at the end of time there will be a physical bodily resurrection of the dead after which God would raise the righteous to eternal life and the wicked to judgement.

Martha's faith taught her to hope in God. She believed that her brother would rise again someday. She even believed that Jesus was God's Messiah. However, she was completely unprepared for what Jesus did. In raising Lazarus from the dead Jesus was proving beyond a shadow of a doubt that He was sent by God and held the keys to life and death. Even people who had believed in Jesus already were stunned by this display of His power.

- *Why do you think Jesus cried when He knew that He would that He would soon bring Lazarus back to life?*
- *Have you ever had a near-death experience? How did it affect you?*
- *What do you think of people who claim to have had post-death experiences?*
- *What do you think happens after death? What would you take to be conclusive evidence that there is in fact life after death?*

[45] Therefore many of the Jews who came to Mary, and saw what He had done, believed in Him. [46] But some of them went to the Pharisees and told them the things which Jesus had done.

[47] Therefore the chief priests and the Pharisees convened a council, and were saying, "What are we doing? For this man is performing many signs. [48] If we let Him *go on* like this, all men will believe in Him, and the Romans will come and take away both our place and our nation." [49] But one of them, Caiaphas, who was high priest that year, said to them, "You know nothing at all, [50] nor do you take into account that it is expedient for you that one man die for the people, and that the whole nation not perish." [51] Now he did not say this on his own initiative, but being high priest that year, he prophesied that Jesus was going to die for the nation, [52] and not for the nation only, but in order that He might also gather together into one the children of God who are scattered abroad. [53] So from that day on they planned together to kill Him.

[54] Therefore Jesus no longer continued to walk publicly among the Jews, but went away from there to the country near the wilderness, into a city called Ephraim; and there He stayed with the disciples.

⁵⁵ Now the Passover of the Jews was near, and many went up to Jerusalem out of the country before the Passover to purify themselves.⁵⁶ So they were seeking for Jesus, and were saying to one another as they stood in the temple, "What do you think; that He will not come to the feast at all?" ⁵⁷ Now the chief priests and the Pharisees had given orders that if anyone knew where He was, he was to report it, so that they might seize Him.

12 Jesus, therefore, six days before the Passover, came to Bethany where Lazarus was, whom Jesus had raised from the dead. ² So they made Him a supper there, and Martha was serving; but Lazarus was one of those reclining *at the table* with Him. ³ Mary then took a pound of very costly perfume of pure nard, and anointed the feet of Jesus and wiped His feet with her hair; and the house was filled with the fragrance of the perfume. ⁴ But Judas Iscariot, one of His disciples, who was intending to betray Him, said, ⁵ "Why was this perfume not sold for three hundred denarii and given to poor *people*?" ⁶ Now he said this, not because he was concerned about the poor, but because he was a thief, and as he had the money box, he used to pilfer what was put into it. ⁷ Therefore Jesus said, "Let her alone, so that she may keep it for the day of My burial. ⁸ For you always have the poor with you, but you do not always have Me."

⁹ The large crowd of the Jews then learned that He was there; and they came, not for Jesus' sake only, but that they might also see Lazarus, whom He raised from the dead. ¹⁰ But the chief priests planned to put Lazarus to death also; ¹¹ because on account of him many of the Jews were going away and were believing in Jesus.

¹² On the next day the large crowd who had come to the feast, when they heard that Jesus was coming to Jerusalem, ¹³ took the branches of the palm trees and went out to meet Him, and *began* to shout, "Hosanna!ʸ BLESSED IS HE WHO COMES IN THE NAME OF

ʸ *Hosanna!* "Hosanna" means ""Save us now!" – the people understood that Jesus came to save them.

THE LORD, even the King of Israel." [14] Jesus, finding a young donkey, sat on it; as it is written, [15] "FEAR NOT, DAUGHTER OF ZION; BEHOLD, YOUR KING IS COMING, SEATED ON A DONKEY'S COLT." [16] These things His disciples did not understand at the first; but when Jesus was glorified, then they remembered that these things were written of Him, and that they had done these things to Him. [17] So the people, who were with Him when He called Lazarus out of the tomb and raised him from the dead, continued to testify *about Him*. [18] For this reason also the people went and met Him, because they heard that He had performed this sign. [19] So the Pharisees said to one another, "You see that you are not doing any good; look, the world has gone after Him."

[20] Now there were some Greeks among those who were going up to worship at the feast; [21] these then came to Philip, who was from Bethsaida of Galilee, and *began to* ask him, saying, "Sir, we wish to see Jesus." [22] Philip came and told Andrew; Andrew and Philip came and told Jesus. [23] And Jesus answered them, saying, "The hour has come for the Son of Man to be glorified. [24] Truly, truly, I say to you, unless a grain of wheat falls into the earth and dies, it remains alone; but if it dies, it bears much fruit. [25] He who loves his life loses it, and he who hates his life in this world will keep it to life eternal. [26] If anyone serves Me, he must follow Me; and where I am, there My servant will be also; if anyone serves Me, the Father will honor him.

[27] "Now My soul has become troubled; and what shall I say, 'Father, save Me from this hour'? But for this purpose I came to this hour. [28] Father, glorify Your name." Then a voice came out of heaven: "I have both glorified it, and will glorify it again." [29] So the crowd *of people* who stood by and heard it were saying that it had thundered; others were saying, "An angel has spoken to Him." [30] Jesus answered and said, "This voice has not come for My sake, but for your sakes. [31] Now judgment is upon this world; now the ruler of this world will be cast out. [32] And I, if I am lifted up from the earth, will draw all men

to Myself." ³³ But He was saying this to indicate the kind of death by which He was to die. ³⁴ The crowd then answered Him, "We have heard out of the Law that the Christ is to remain forever; and how can You say, 'The Son of Man must be lifted up'? Who is this Son of Man?" ³⁵ So Jesus said to them, "For a little while longer the Light is among you. Walk while you have the Light, so that darkness will not overtake you; he who walks in the darkness does not know where he goes. ³⁶ While you have the Light, believe in the Light, so that you may become sons of Light."

These things Jesus spoke, and He went away and hid Himself from them. ³⁷ But though He had performed so many signs before them, *yet* they were not believing in Him. ³⁸ *This was* to fulfill the word of Isaiah the prophet which he spoke: "LORD, WHO HAS BELIEVED OUR REPORT? AND TO WHOM HAS THE ARM OF THE LORD BEEN REVEALED?" ³⁹ For this reason they could not believe, for Isaiah said again, ⁴⁰ "HE HAS BLINDED THEIR EYES AND HE HARDENED THEIR HEART, SO THAT THEY WOULD NOT SEE WITH THEIR EYES AND PERCEIVE WITH THEIR HEART, AND BE CONVERTED AND I HEAL THEM." ⁴¹ These things Isaiah said because he saw His glory, and he spoke of Him. ⁴² Nevertheless many even of the rulers believed in Him, but because of the Pharisees they were not confessing *Him*, for fear that they would be put out of the synagogue; ⁴³ for they loved the approval of men rather than the approval of God.

⁴⁴ And Jesus cried out and said, "He who believes in Me, does not believe in Me but in Him who sent Me. ⁴⁵ He who sees Me sees the One who sent Me. ⁴⁶ I have come *as* Light into the world, so that everyone who believes in Me will not remain in darkness. ⁴⁷ If anyone hears My sayings and does not keep them, I do not judge him; for I did not come to judge the world, but to save the world. ⁴⁸ He who rejects Me and does not receive My sayings, has one who judges him; the word I spoke is what will judge him at the last day. ⁴⁹ For I did not speak on My own initiative, but the Father Himself who sent Me has given Me a commandment *as to* what to say and what to speak.

50 I know that His commandment is eternal life; therefore the things I speak, I speak just as the Father has told Me."

13 Now before the Feast of the Passover, Jesus knowing that His hour had come that He would depart out of this world to the Father, having loved His own who were in the world, He loved them to the end. **2** During supper, the devil having already put into the heart of Judas Iscariot, *the son* of Simon, to betray Him, **3** *Jesus*, knowing that the Father had given all things into His hands, and that He had come forth from God and was going back to God, **4** got up from supper, and laid aside His garments; and taking a towel, He girded Himself.

5 Then He poured water into the basin, and began to wash the disciples' feet[z] and to wipe them with the towel with which He was girded. **6** So He came to Simon Peter. He said to Him, "Lord, do You wash my feet?" **7** Jesus answered and said to him, "What I do you do not realize now, but you will understand hereafter." **8** Peter said to Him, "Never shall You wash my feet!" Jesus answered him, "If I do not wash you, you have no part with Me." **9** Simon Peter said to Him, "Lord, *then wash* not only my feet, but also my hands and my head." **10** Jesus said to him, "He who has bathed needs only to wash his feet, but is completely clean; and you are clean, but not all *of you*." **11** For He knew the one who was betraying Him; for this reason He said, "Not all of you are clean."

12 So when He had washed their feet, and taken His garments and reclined *at the table* again, He said to them, "Do you know what I have done to you? **13** You call Me Teacher and Lord; and you are right, for *so* I am. **14** If I then, the Lord and the Teacher, washed your feet, you also ought to wash one another's feet. **15** For I gave you an example that you also should do as I did to you. **16** Truly, truly, I say to you, a

---

[z] *To wash the disciples' feet*: It was proper custom when entering a house to wash one's feet. usually, one would wash his own feet. In rare cases, a servant might wash them for you. Jesus was giving them a profound example of how they were to serve one another in humility and love.

slave is not greater than his master, nor *is* one who is sent greater than the one who sent him. ¹⁷ If you know these things, you are blessed if you do them.¹⁸ I do not speak of all of you. I know the ones I have chosen; but *it is* that the Scripture may be fulfilled, 'HE WHO EATS MY BREAD HAS LIFTED UP HIS HEEL AGAINST ME.' ¹⁹ From now on I am telling you before *it* comes to pass, so that when it does occur, you may believe that I am *He*. ²⁰ Truly, truly, I say to you, he who receives whomever I send receives Me; and he who receives Me receives Him who sent Me."

²¹ When Jesus had said this, He became troubled in spirit, and testified and said, "Truly, truly, I say to you, that one of you will betray Me."²² The disciples *began* looking at one another, at a loss *to know* of which one He was speaking. ²³ There was reclining on Jesus' bosom one of His disciples, whom Jesus loved. ²⁴ So Simon Peter gestured to him, and said to him, "Tell *us* who it is of whom He is speaking." ²⁵ He, leaning back thus on Jesus' bosom, said to Him, "Lord, who is it?" ²⁶ Jesus then answered, "That is the one for whom I shall dip the morsel and give it to him." So when He had dipped the morsel, He took and gave it to Judas, *the son* of Simon Iscariot. ²⁷ After the morsel, Satan then entered into him. Therefore Jesus said to him, "What you do, do quickly." ²⁸ Now no one of those reclining *at the table* knew for what purpose He had said this to him. ²⁹ For some were supposing, because Judas had the money box, that Jesus was saying to him, "Buy the things we have need of for the feast"; or else, that he should give something to the poor. ³⁰ So after receiving the morsel he went out immediately; and it was night.

³¹ Therefore when he had gone out, Jesus said, "Now is the Son of Man glorified, and God is glorified in Him; ³² if God is glorified in Him, God will also glorify Him in Himself, and will glorify Him immediately.³³ Little children, I am with you a little while longer. You will seek Me; and as I said to the Jews, now I also say to you, 'Where I am going, you cannot come.' ³⁴ A new commandment I give to you, that you love one another, even as I have loved you, that you also

love one another. ³⁵ By this all men will know that you are My disciples, if you have love for one another."

³⁶ Simon Peter said to Him, "Lord, where are You going?" Jesus answered, "Where I go, you cannot follow Me now; but you will follow later." ³⁷ Peter said to Him, "Lord, why can I not follow You right now? I will lay down my life for You." ³⁸ Jesus answered, "Will you lay down your life for Me? Truly, truly, I say to you, a rooster will not crow until you deny Me three times.

☛ Guidepost 7

Jesus is the Way, the Truth and the Life ("I Am" statement 6)

14 "Let not your hearts be troubled. Believe in God; believe also in me. ² In my Father's house are many rooms. If it were not so, would I have told you that I go to prepare a place for you? ³ And if I go and prepare a place for you, I will come again and will take you to myself, that where I am you may be also. ⁴ And you know the way to where I am going." ⁵ Thomas said to him, "Lord, we do not know where you are going. How can we know the way?" ⁶ Jesus said to him, "I am the way, and the truth, and the life. No one comes to the Father except through me. ⁷ If you had known me, you would have known my Father also. From now on you do know him and have seen him."

⁸ Philip said to him, "Lord, show us the Father, and it is enough for us."⁹ Jesus said to him, "Have I been with you so long, and you still do not know me, Philip? Whoever has seen me has seen the Father. How can you say, 'Show us the Father'? ¹⁰ Do you not believe that I am in the Father and the Father is in me? The words that I say to you I do not speak on my own authority, but the Father who dwells in me does his works.

☛ Discussion 7
What does this guidepost teach about Jesus?

Perhaps no claim of Jesus' upsets people more in this day and age as His claim to be the only way to God: "no one comes to the Father but by me." This is an offensive statement to many today who hold to some form of religious pluralism. Religious pluralism is the belief that the various religious belief systems are merely different paths leading to God. Often the analogy of a mountain is used: just as there may be many paths at the foot of the mountain, in the end they all lead to the top.

Yet three major problems exist within this analogy. The first is that the religions themselves hold to different, even contradictory, understandings of God/god. We are not merely on different paths, we are climbing different mountains. The second is that the climber who sets out at the foot of the mountain really has no assurance that the path they are on will lead to the top. The path may be washed out, double-back, or be blocked in some way. Only with guidance from someone who has descended from the peak can there be assurance that their path will lead them to the desired destination. The third problem is that religious pluralism is self-defeating, for in denying the absolute authority of any world view, it begs the question of why its own view should be taken as absolute.

So what keeps us from drifting into total relativity? This is the heart of the astounding claim Jesus makes: He alone has come from the Father to show us the way to the Father.

He in fact is the Way, meaning that we come to the Father through Jesus, for Jesus alone perfectly represents the Father and reveals Him to us. If Jesus is who He claimed to be, then the problem of relativity is solved and our path up the mountain to God is clear.

- *How does the idea of revelation (guidance from the top of the mountain) solve the problem of relativity (not knowing where any particular path leads)?*
- *You have been given the opportunity to know and accept Jesus. Should the idea that some other people have not had this opportunity affect your decision?*
- *Others have claimed to speak on behalf of God. Why might someone believe that Jesus is qualitatively different from those who came before or after him?*

---

[11] Believe me," he said to them all, "when I say that I am in the Father and the Father in me, or else believe me because of the work itself. [12]In truth I say to you, the person who believes in me will themselves do the work that I am doing. They will do greater work still, because I am going to the Father.

[13] Whatever you ask, in my name, I will do, so that the Father may be honored in the Son. [14] If you ask anything, in my name, I will do it. [15]If you love me, you will keep my commandments, [16] and I will ask the Father, and he will give you another Helper, to be with you always – the Spirit of truth. [17] The world cannot receive this Spirit, because it does not see him or recognize him, but you recognize him, because he is always with you, and is within you. [18] I will not leave you as orphans; I will come to you. [19]In a little while the world will see me no more, but you will still see me. Because I live, you will live also. [20] At that time you will recognize that I am in the Father, and you in me, and I in you. [21] Those who have my commands and keep them love me; and the person who loves me will be loved by my Father, and I will love them, and will reveal myself to them."

[22] "How is it, Lord, that you are going to reveal yourself to us, and not to the world?" said Judas (not Judas Iscariot - a different Judas). [23] "Whoever loves me," Jesus answered, "will keep my word, and my Father will love him, and we will come to him and make our home with him. [24] The person who does not love me will not keep my word.

For this is not my own word, but comes from the Father who sent me.

⚑ Guidepost 8
Jesus is the True Vine
("I Am" Statement #7)

25 "These things I have spoken to you while I am still with you. 26 But the Helper, the Holy Spirit, whom the Father will send in my name, he will teach you all things and bring to your remembrance all that I have said to you. 27 Peace I leave with you; my peace I give to you. Not as the world gives do I give to you. Let not your hearts be troubled, neither let them be afraid. 28 You heard me say to you, 'I am going away, and I will come to you.' If you loved me, you would have rejoiced, because I am going to the Father, for the Father is greater than I. 29 And now I have told you before it takes place, so that when it does take place you may believe. 30 I will no longer talk much with you, for the ruler of this world is coming. He has no claim on me, 31 but I do as the Father has commanded me, so that the world may know that I love the Father. Rise, let us go from here.

15 "I am the true vine, and my Father is the vinedresser. 2 Every branch in me that does not bear fruit he takes away, and every branch that does bear fruit he prunes, that it may bear more fruit. 3 Already you are clean because of the word that I have spoken to you. 4 Abide in me, and I in you. As the branch cannot bear fruit by itself, unless it abides in the vine, neither can you, unless you abide in me. 5 I am the vine; you are the branches. Whoever abides in me and I in him, he it is that bears much fruit, for apart from me you can do nothing. 6 If anyone does not abide in me he is thrown away like a branch and withers; and the branches are gathered, thrown into the fire, and burned. 7 If you abide in me, and my words abide in you, ask whatever you wish, and it will be done for you. [8] By this my Father is glorified, that you bear much fruit and so prove to be my disciples. [9] As the Father has loved me, so have I loved you. Abide in my love. [10] If you keep my commandments, you will abide in my love, just as I have kept my Father's commandments and abide in his love. [11] These things I have spoken to you, that my joy may be in you, and that your joy may be full.

[12] "This is my commandment, that you love one another as I have loved you. [13] Greater love has no one than this, that someone lay down his life for his friends. [14] You are my friends if you do what I command you.[15] No longer do I call you servants, for the servant does not know what his master is doing; but I have called you friends, for all that I have heard from my Father I have made known to you. [16] You did not choose me, but I chose you and appointed you that you should go and bear fruit and that your fruit should abide, so that whatever you ask the Father in my name, he may give it to you. [17] These things I command you, so that you will love one another.

✝ Discussion 8
What does this guidepost teach about Jesus?

While most of the Book of John is directed toward people who are still deciding whether or not to believe in Jesus, Jesus' words on the night before his death are directed to those who have come to believe in Him. Jesus reassures them that though He will soon leave them to return to the Father, He would not leave them entirely alone, for He would send them God's Spirit. The Holy Spirit would come to live in them as a guiding and empowering presence. Through the power of the Holy Spirit, believers in Jesus will produce great works of love and experience joy and peace. Yet we have all met people who claim to be Christians that do not

---

reflect this sort of love, joy or peace. Certainly, throughout history many terrible acts have been done in the name of Christ. How can this be?

Here we must notice that Jesus does not promise that all who merely *claim* his name will produce fruit, we must abide in Him and He in us. To abide in Him means that we remain faithful to His teachings, particularly that we obey his commandment of love. To have Him abide in us means that we live lives open to the guidance of His Holy Spirit. This then is what distinguishes a true Christian: they produce fruit consistent with the love of God.

- *What is the difference between claiming to be a follower of Jesus and truly abiding in Christ?*
- *Do you think it is fair to judge Christianity on the actions of those who claim to be Christians?*
- *What has been your experience in dealing with Christians? Have you found that they have genuinely reflected Christ's life and teachings, or are only Christian in name?*
- *If you are a Christian, how do you ensure that you are abiding in Christ and He in you?*

[18] "If the world hates you, you know that it has hated Me before *it hated* you. [19] If you were of the world, the world would love its own; but because you are not of the world, but I chose you out of the world, because of this the world hates you. [20] Remember the word that I said to you, 'A slave is not greater than his master.' If they persecuted Me, they will also persecute you; if they kept My word, they will keep yours also.[21] But all these things they will do to you for My name's sake, because they do not know the One who sent Me. [22] If I had not come and spoken to them, they would not have sin, but now they have no excuse for their sin. [23] He who hates Me hates My Father also. [24] If I had not done among them the works which no one else did, they would not have sin; but now they have both seen

and hated Me and My Father as well.²⁵ But *they have done this* to fulfill the word that is written in their Law, 'THEY HATED ME WITHOUT A CAUSE.'

²⁶ "When the Helper comes, whom I will send to you from the Father, *that is* the Spirit of truth who proceeds from the Father, He will testify about Me, ²⁷ and you *will* testify also, because you have been with Me from the beginning.

16 "These things I have spoken to you so that you may be kept from stumbling. ² They will make you outcasts from the synagogue, but an hour is coming for everyone who kills you to think that he is offering service to God. ³ These things they will do because they have not known the Father or Me. ⁴ But these things I have spoken to you, so that when their hour comes, you may remember that I told you of them. These things I did not say to you at the beginning, because I was with you.

⁵ "But now I am going to Him who sent Me; and none of you asks Me, 'Where are You going?' ⁶ But because I have said these things to you, sorrow has filled your heart. ⁷ But I tell you the truth, it is to your advantage that I go away; for if I do not go away, the Helper will not come to you; but if I go, I will send Him to you. ⁸ And He, when He comes, will convict the world concerning sin and righteousness and judgment; ⁹ concerning sin, because they do not believe in Me; ¹⁰ and concerning righteousness, because I go to the Father and you no longer see Me; ¹¹ and concerning judgment, because the ruler of this world has been judged.

¹² "I have many more things to say to you, but you cannot bear *them* now. ¹³ But when He, the Spirit of truth, comes, He will guide you into all the truth; for He will not speak on His own initiative, but whatever He hears, He will speak; and He will disclose to you what is to come. ¹⁴ He will glorify Me, for He will take of Mine and will disclose *it* to you. ¹⁵ All things that the Father has are Mine; therefore I said that He takes of Mine and will disclose *it* to you.

16 "A little while, and you will no longer see Me; and again a little while, and you will see Me." 17 *Some* of His disciples then said to one another, "What is this thing He is telling us, 'A little while, and you will not see Me; and again a little while, and you will see Me'; and, 'because I go to the Father'?" 18 So they were saying, "What is this that He says, 'A little while'? We do not know what He is talking about." 19 Jesus knew that they wished to question Him, and He said to them, "Are you deliberating together about this, that I said, 'A little while, and you will not see Me, and again a little while, and you will see Me'? 20 Truly, truly, I say to you, that you will weep and lament, but the world will rejoice; you will grieve, but your grief will be turned into joy. 21 Whenever a woman is in labor she has pain, because her hour has come; but when she gives birth to the child, she no longer remembers the anguish because of the joy that a child has been born into the world. 22 Therefore you too have grief now; but I will see you again, and your heart will rejoice, and no one *will* take your joy away from you.

23 In that day you will not question Me about anything. Truly, truly, I say to you, if you ask the Father for anything in My name, He will give it to you. 24 Until now you have asked for nothing in My name; ask and you will receive, so that your joy may be made full.

25 "These things I have spoken to you in figurative language; an hour is coming when I will no longer speak to you in figurative language, but will tell you plainly of the Father. 26 In that day you will ask in My name, and I do not say to you that I will request of the Father on your behalf; 27 for the Father Himself loves you, because you have loved Me and have believed that I came forth from the Father. 28 I came forth from the Father and have come into the world; I am leaving the world again and going to the Father."

29 His disciples said, "Lo, now You are speaking plainly and are not using a figure of speech. 30 Now we know that You know all things, and have no need for anyone to question You; by this we believe that You came from God." 31 Jesus answered them, "Do you now believe?32 Behold, an hour is coming, and has *already* come, for

you to be scattered, each to his own *home*, and to leave Me alone; and *yet* I am not alone, because the Father is with Me. ³³ These things I have spoken to you, so that in Me you may have peace. In the world you have tribulation, but take courage; I have overcome the world."

17 Jesus spoke these things; and lifting up His eyes to heaven, He said, "Father, the hour has come; glorify Your Son, that the Son may glorify You, ² even as You gave Him authority over all flesh, that to all whom You have given Him, He may give eternal life. ³ This is eternal life, that they may know You, the only true God, and Jesus Christ whom You have sent. ⁴ I glorified You on the earth, having accomplished the work which You have given Me to do. ⁵ Now, Father, glorify Me together with Yourself, with the glory which I had with You before the world was.

⁶ "I have manifested Your name to the men whom You gave Me out of the world; they were Yours and You gave them to Me, and they have kept Your word. ⁷ Now they have come to know that everything You have given Me is from You; ⁸ for the words which You gave Me I have given to them; and they received *them* and truly understood that I came forth from You, and they believed that You sent Me. ⁹ I ask on their behalf; I do not ask on behalf of the world, but of those whom You have given Me; for they are Yours; ¹⁰ and all things that are Mine are Yours, and Yours are Mine; and I have been glorified in them. ¹¹ I am no longer in the world; and *yet* they themselves are in the world, and I come to You. Holy Father, keep them in Your name, *the name* which You have given Me, that they may be one even as We *are*. ¹² While I was with them, I was keeping them in Your name which You have given Me; and I guarded them and not one of them perished but the son of perdition, so that the Scripture would be fulfilled.

¹³ But now I come to You; and these things I speak in the world so that they may have My joy made full in themselves. ¹⁴ I have given them Your word; and the world has hated them, because they are not of the world, even as I am not of the world. ¹⁵ I do not ask You to

take them out of the world, but to keep them from the evil *one*. ¹⁶ They are not of the world, even as I am not of the world. ¹⁷ Sanctify them in the truth; Your word is truth. ¹⁸ As You sent Me into the world, I also have sent them into the world. ¹⁹ For their sakes I sanctify Myself, that they themselves also may be sanctified in truth.

²⁰ "I do not ask on behalf of these alone, but for those also who believe in Me through their word; ²¹ that they may all be one; even as You, Father, *are* in Me and I in You, that they also may be in Us, so that the world may believe that You sent Me.

²² The glory which You have given Me I have given to them, that they may be one, just as We are one; ²³ I in them and You in Me, that they may be perfected in unity, so that the world may know that You sent Me, and loved them, even as You have loved Me. ²⁴ Father, I desire that they also, whom You have given Me, be with Me where I am, so that they may see My glory which You have given Me, for You loved Me before the foundation of the world.

²⁵ "O righteous Father, although the world has not known You, yet I have known You; and these have known that You sent Me; ²⁶ and I have made Your name known to them, and will make it known, so that the love with which You loved Me may be in them, and I in them."

18 When Jesus had spoken these words, He went forth with His disciples over the ravine of the Kidron, where there was a garden, in which He entered with His disciples. ² Now Judas also, who was betraying Him, knew the place, for Jesus had often met there with His disciples. ³ Judas then, having received the *Roman* cohort and officers from the chief priests and the Pharisees, came there with lanterns and torches and weapons. ⁴ So Jesus, knowing all the things that were coming upon Him, went forth and said to them, "Whom do you seek?" ⁵ They answered Him, "Jesus the Nazarene." He said to them, "I am *He*." And Judas also, who was betraying Him, was standing with them. ⁶ So when He said to them, "I am *He*," they drew back and fell to the ground. ⁷ Therefore He again asked them, "Whom do you seek?" And they said, "Jesus the Nazarene." [8] Jesus answered, "I told you that I am *He*; so if you seek Me, let these go their way," [9] to fulfill the word which He spoke, "Of those whom You have given Me I lost not one." [10] Simon Peter then, having a sword, drew it and struck the high priest's slave, and cut off his right ear; and the slave's name was Malchus. [11] So Jesus said to Peter, "Put the sword into the sheath; the cup which the Father has given Me, shall I not drink it?"

[12] So the *Roman* cohort and the commander and the officers of the Jews, arrested Jesus and bound Him, [13] and led Him to Annas first; for he was father-in-law of Caiaphas, who was high priest that year. [14] Now Caiaphas was the one who had advised the Jews that it was expedient for one man to die on behalf of the people.

[15] Simon Peter was following Jesus, and *so was* another disciple. Now that disciple was known to the high priest, and entered with Jesus into the court of the high priest, [16] but Peter was standing at the door outside. So the other disciple, who was known to the high priest, went out and spoke to the doorkeeper, and brought Peter in. [17] Then the slave-girl who kept the door said to Peter, "You are not also *one* of this man's disciples, are you?" He said, "I am not." [18] Now the slaves and the officers were standing *there*, having made a charcoal fire, for it was cold and they were warming themselves; and Peter was also with them, standing and warming himself.

[19] The high priest then questioned Jesus about His disciples, and about His teaching. [20] Jesus answered him, "I have spoken openly to the world; I always taught in synagogues and in the temple, where all the Jews come together; and I spoke nothing in secret. [21] Why do you question Me? Question those who have heard what I spoke to them; they know what I said." [22] When He had said this, one of the officers standing nearby struck Jesus, saying, "Is that the way You answer the high priest?" [23] Jesus answered him, "If I have spoken wrongly, testify of the wrong; but if rightly, why do you strike Me?" [24] So Annas sent Him bound to Caiaphas the high priest.

[25] Now Simon Peter was standing and warming himself. So they said to him, "You are not also *one* of His disciples, are you?" He

denied *it*, and said, "I am not." ²⁶ One of the slaves of the high priest, being a relative of the one whose ear Peter cut off, said, "Did I not see you in the garden with Him?" ²⁷ Peter then denied *it* again, and immediately a rooster crowed.

²⁸ Then they led Jesus from Caiaphas into the Praetorium, and it was early; and they themselves did not enter into the Praetorium so that they would not be defiled, but might eat the Passover. ²⁹ Therefore Pilate^{aa} went out to them and said, "What accusation do you bring against this Man?" ³⁰ They answered and said to him, "If this Man were not an evildoer, we would not have delivered Him to you." ³¹ So Pilate said to them, "Take Him yourselves, and judge Him according to your law." The Jews said to him, "We are not permitted to put anyone to death," ³² to fulfill the word of Jesus which He spoke, signifying by what kind of death He was about to die.

⭢ Guidepost 9
Jesus Was Killed Because He Claimed to be the Son of God

³³ So Pilate entered his headquarters again and called Jesus and said to him, "Are you the King of the Jews?" ³⁴ Jesus answered, "Do you say this of your own accord, or did others say it to you about me?" ³⁵ Pilate answered, "Am I a Jew? Your own nation and the chief priests have delivered you over to me. What have you done?" ³⁶ Jesus answered, "My kingdom is not of this world. If my kingdom were of this world, my servants would have been fighting, that I might not be delivered over to the Jews. But my kingdom is not from the world." ³⁷ Then Pilate said to him, "So you are a king?" Jesus answered, "You say that I am a king. For this purpose I was born and for this purpose

---

^{aa} *Pilate*: Pontius Pilate was governor of Judea during the latter years of Jesus' lifetime. He represented the Roman occupation in Judea, and as such was committed to keeping the peace and quashing any movement that could potentially disturb the social order.

I have come into the world—to bear witness to the truth. Everyone who is of the truth listens to my voice." **38** Pilate said to him, "What is truth?"

After he had said this, he went back outside to the Jews and told them, "I find no guilt in him. **39** But you have a custom that I should release one man for you at the Passover. So do you want me to release to you the King of the Jews?" **40** They cried out again, "Not this man, but Barabbas!" Now Barabbas was a robber.

19 Then Pilate took Jesus and flogged him. **2** And the soldiers twisted together a crown of thorns and put it on his head and arrayed him in a purple robe. **3** They came up to him, saying, "Hail, King of the Jews!" and struck him with their hands. **4** Pilate went out again and said to them, "See, I am bringing him out to you that you may know that I find no guilt in him." **5** So Jesus came out, wearing the crown of thorns and the purple robe. Pilate said to them, "Behold the man!" **6** When the chief priests and the officers saw him, they cried out, "Crucify him, crucify him!" Pilate said to them, "Take him yourselves and crucify him, for I find no guilt in him." **7** The Jews answered him, "We have a law, and according to that law he ought to die because he has made himself the Son of God."

✝ Discussion 9
What does this guidepost teach about Jesus?

The scriptures are absolutely clear in their testimony: Jesus was sentenced to death because He claimed to be the Son of God. To the Jewish leaders of the day this was a blasphemous claim of the sort that called for the full punishment of the law. Pilate, of course, was concerned with maintaining Roman rule and order,

---

yet even he was satisfied that Jesus did not pose a political threat. Jesus made it very clear that He was not seeking to build an earthly kingdom or start a rebellion. He broke no law, legal or moral, yet was sentenced to death because of His claim to be the Son of God. This is what so offended the people of His day, and this is still what offends people to this day.

Many today believe Jesus to be a good man, a moral teacher, or a prophet. They do not believe Jesus to have claimed anything more than this for himself. Yet those who believe in *that* Jesus have a hard time explaining why people were so bent on killing him. What was it about Jesus that caused such a violent response? Jesus left us little room to merely write him off as a generally good, though misguided, man. Either He was who He claimed to be, and therefore to be worshipped as God, or He was at best a lunatic or at worst a conman. He left us no middle ground; either Jesus is who He claimed to be, or He is not. We are all in the position of Pilate, thinking we are in the position to judge Jesus. However, if what Jesus claimed about Himself is true, we do not stand over Him in judgment, but He stands over us.

- *What is it about Jesus that caused such strong reactions to Him? Do you think that Jesus still causes similar reactions today?*
- *If you were Pilate, what factors would you have weighed in your decision to either condemn or free Jesus?*
- *Even though Pilate found no guilt in Jesus, he was still swayed by the crowd to hand Jesus over to be crucified. How much do other peoples' reactions to Jesus sway your opinion of Him?*

8 Therefore when Pilate heard this statement, he was *even* more afraid;**9** and he entered into the Praetorium again and said to Jesus, "Where are You from?" But Jesus gave him no answer. **10** So Pilate said to Him, "You do not speak to me? Do You not know that I have authority to release You, and I have authority to crucify You?" **11** Jesus answered, "You would have no authority over Me, unless it had been given you from above; for this reason he who delivered Me to you has *the* greater sin." **12** As a result of this Pilate made efforts to release Him, but the Jews cried out saying, "If you release this Man, you are no friend of Caesar; everyone who makes himself out *to be* a king opposes Caesar."

13 Therefore when Pilate heard these words, he brought Jesus out, and sat down on the judgment seat at a place called The Pavement, but in Hebrew, Gabbatha. **14** Now it was the day of preparation for the Passover; it was about the sixth hour. And he said to the Jews, "Behold, your King!" **15** So they cried out, "Away with *Him*, away with *Him*, crucify Him!" Pilate said to them, "Shall I crucify your King?" The chief priests answered, "We have no king but Caesar."

16 So he then handed Him over to them to be crucified.

17 They took Jesus, therefore, and He went out, bearing His own cross, to the place called the Place of a Skull, which is called in Hebrew, Golgotha. **18** There they crucified Him, and with Him two other men, one on either side, and Jesus in between. **19** Pilate also wrote an inscription and put it on the cross. It was written, "JESUS THE NAZARENE, THE KING OF THE JEWS." **20** Therefore many of the Jews read this inscription, for the place where Jesus was crucified was near the city; and it was written in Hebrew, Latin *and* in Greek. **21** So the chief priests of the Jews were saying to Pilate, "Do not write, 'The King of the Jews'; but that He said, 'I am King of the Jews.'" **22** Pilate answered, "What I have written I have written."

23 Then the soldiers, when they had crucified Jesus, took His outer garments and made four parts, a part to every soldier and *also* the tunic; now the tunic was seamless, woven in one piece. **24** So they said to one another, "Let us not tear it, but cast lots for it, *to decide* whose it shall be"; *this was* to fulfill the Scripture: "THEY DIVIDED MY OUTER GARMENTS AMONG THEM, AND FOR MY CLOTHING THEY CAST LOTS."[25] Therefore the soldiers did these things.

But standing by the cross of Jesus were His mother, and His mother's sister, Mary the *wife* of Clopas, and Mary Magdalene. [26] When Jesus then saw His mother, and the disciple whom He loved standing nearby, He said to His mother, "Woman, behold, your son!" [27] Then He said to the disciple, "Behold, your mother!" From that hour the disciple took her into his own *household*.

[28] After this, Jesus, knowing that all things had already been accomplished, to fulfill the Scripture, said, "I am thirsty." [29] A jar full of sour wine was standing there; so they put a sponge full of the sour wine upon *a branch of* hyssop and brought it up to His mouth. [30] Therefore when Jesus had received the sour wine, He said, "It is finished!" And He bowed His head and gave up His spirit.

[31] Then the Jews, because it was the day of preparation, so that the bodies would not remain on the cross on the Sabbath (for that Sabbath was a high day), asked Pilate that their legs might be broken, and *that* they might be taken away. [32] So the soldiers came, and broke the legs of the first man and of the other who was crucified with Him;[33] but coming to Jesus, when they saw that He was already dead, they did not break His legs. [34] But one of the soldiers pierced His side with a spear, and immediately blood and water came out. [35] And he who has seen has testified, and his testimony is true; and he knows that he is telling the truth, so that you also may believe. [36] For these things came to pass to fulfill the Scripture, "NOT A BONE OF HIM SHALL BE BROKEN."[37] And again another Scripture says, "THEY SHALL LOOK ON HIM WHOM THEY PIERCED."

[38] After these things Joseph of Arimathea, being a disciple of Jesus, but a secret *one* for fear of the Jews, asked Pilate that he might take away the body of Jesus; and Pilate granted permission. So he came and took away His body. [39] Nicodemus, who had first come to Him by night, also came, bringing a mixture of myrrh and aloes, about a hundred pounds *weight*. [40] So they took the body of Jesus and bound

it in linen wrappings with the spices, as is the burial custom of the Jews. [41] Now in the place where He was crucified there was a garden, and in the garden a new tomb in which no one had yet been laid. [42] Therefore because of the Jewish day of preparation, since the tomb was nearby, they laid Jesus there.

20 Now on the first *day* of the week Mary Magdalene came early to the tomb, while it was still dark, and saw the stone *already* taken away from the tomb. [2] So she ran and came to Simon Peter and to the other disciple whom Jesus loved, and said to them, "They have taken away the Lord out of the tomb, and we do not know where they have laid Him." [3] So Peter and the other disciple went forth, and they were going to the tomb. [4] The two were running together; and the other disciple ran ahead faster than Peter and came to the tomb first; [5] and stooping and looking in, he saw the linen wrappings lying *there*; but he did not go in. [6] And so Simon Peter also came, following him, and entered the tomb; and he saw the linen wrappings lying *there*, [7] and the face-cloth which had been on His head, not lying with the linen wrappings, but rolled up in a place by itself. [8] So the other disciple who had first come to the tomb then also entered, and he saw and believed. [9] For as yet they did not understand the Scripture, that He must rise again from the dead. [10] So the disciples went away again to their own homes.

[11] But Mary was standing outside the tomb weeping; and so, as she wept, she stooped and looked into the tomb; [12] and she saw two angels in white sitting, one at the head and one at the feet, where the body of Jesus had been lying. [13] And they said to her, "Woman, why are you weeping?" She said to them, "Because they have taken away my Lord, and I do not know where they have laid Him." [14] When she had said this, she turned around and saw Jesus standing *there*, and did not know that it was Jesus. [15] Jesus said to her, "Woman, why are you weeping? Whom are you seeking?" Supposing Him to be the gardener, she said to Him, "Sir, if you have carried Him away, tell me where you have laid Him, and I will take Him away." [16] Jesus said to

her, "Mary!" She turned and said to Him in Hebrew, "Rabboni!" (which means, Teacher).[17] Jesus said to her, "Stop clinging to Me, for I have not yet ascended to the Father; but go to My brethren and say to them, 'I ascend to My Father and your Father, and My God and your God.'" [18] Mary Magdalene came, announcing to the disciples, "I have seen the Lord," and *that* He had said these things to her.

⭲ Guidepost 10
Jesus Rose from the Dead,
Proving He is Indeed the Messiah

[19] On the evening of that day, the first day of the week, the doors being locked where the disciples were for fear of the Jews, Jesus came and stood among them and said to them, "Peace be with you." [20] When he had said this, he showed them his hands and his side. Then the disciples were glad when they saw the Lord. [21] Jesus said to them again, "Peace be with you. As the Father has sent me, even so I am sending you." [22] And when he had said this, he breathed on them and said to them, "Receive the Holy Spirit. [23] If you forgive the sins of any, they are forgiven them; if you withhold forgiveness from any, it is withheld."

[24] Now Thomas, one of the twelve, called the Twin, was not with them when Jesus came. [25] So the other disciples told him, "We have seen the Lord." But he said to them, "Unless I see in his hands the mark of the nails, and place my finger into the mark of the nails, and place my hand into his side, I will never believe."

[26] Eight days later, his disciples were inside again, and Thomas was with them. Although the doors were locked, Jesus came and stood among them and said, "Peace be with you." [27] Then he said to Thomas, "Put your finger here, and see my hands; and put out your hand, and place it in my side. Do not disbelieve, but believe." [28] Thomas answered him, "My Lord and my God!" [29] Jesus said to

him, "Have you believed because you have seen me? Blessed are those who have not seen and yet have believed."

³⁰ Now Jesus did many other signs in the presence of the disciples, which are not written in this book; ³¹ but these are written so that you may believe that Jesus is the Christ, the Son of God, and that by believing you may have life in his name.

☝ Discussion 10
What does this guidepost teach about Jesus?

Here we come to the climax of the Book of John. Jesus has been raised from the dead just as he foretold. Before His resurrection, one might have written Him off as a nutcase or charlatan, but in rising from the dead, Jesus' most extraordinary claims about Himself were vindicated. It is one thing to say that you are from God and hold the keys to life and death; it is another thing completely to walk out of an empty tomb, alive from the dead.

Yet could it possibly be true? We can all place ourselves in Thomas' position. Will we continue to doubt, or will we believe? Thomas, of course, had the advantage of seeing the risen Christ with his own eyes. Yet John, who was also an eyewitness to the resurrection, begs us to believe in Jesus according to what he has written. It is appropriate for us to demand extraordinary evidence for outlandish claims, and the claim that Christ is the Son of God raised from the dead is perhaps the most outlandish claim ever made. Yet John is confident that his testimony is true and sufficient for us to believe that Christ truly is who He claimed to be. The Christian faith is not a blind faith, but one that rests on the eyewitness testimonies of men who were skeptics like us. It took extraordinary evidence to convince them, yet they were convinced nonetheless.

> - *How do you think Thomas or John would have responded to the charge that faith is incompatible with reason and is, by definition, blind?*
> - *Do you believe that Jesus rose from the dead? What would it take for you to believe that he had?*
> - *If Jesus indeed rose from the dead, how does that verify the claims He made while alive?*
> - *Are you ready to believe in Jesus so that you might have life in His name? See Appendix 1 to learn how you can follow Jesus by faith*

21 After these things Jesus manifested Himself again to the disciples at the Sea of Tiberias, and He manifested *Himself* in this way. ² Simon Peter, and Thomas called Didymus, and Nathanael of Cana in Galilee, and the *sons* of Zebedee, and two others of His disciples were together.³ Simon Peter said to them, "I am going fishing." They said to him, "We will also come with you." They went out and got into the boat; and that night they caught nothing.

⁴ But when the day was now breaking, Jesus stood on the beach; yet the disciples did not know that it was Jesus. ⁵ So Jesus said to them, "Children, you do not have any fish, do you?" They answered Him, "No." ⁶ And He said to them, "Cast the net on the right-hand side of the boat and you will find *a catch*." So they cast, and then they were not able to haul it in because of the great number of fish. ⁷ Therefore that disciple whom Jesus loved said to Peter, "It is the Lord." So when Simon Peter heard that it was the Lord, he put his outer garment on (for he was stripped *for work*), and threw himself into the sea. ⁸ But the other disciples came in the little boat, for they were not far from the land, but about one hundred yards away, dragging the net *full* of fish.

⁹ So when they got out on the land, they saw a charcoal fire *already* laid and fish placed on it, and bread. ¹⁰ Jesus said to them, "Bring

some of the fish which you have now caught." **11** Simon Peter went up and drew the net to land, full of large fish, a hundred and fifty-three; and although there were so many, the net was not torn.

12 Jesus said to them, "Come *and* have breakfast." None of the disciples ventured to question Him, "Who are You?" knowing that it was the Lord. **13** Jesus came and took the bread and gave *it* to them, and the fish likewise. **14** This is now the third time that Jesus was manifested to the disciples, after He was raised from the dead.

15 So when they had finished breakfast, Jesus said to Simon Peter, "Simon, *son* of John, do you love Me more than these?" He said to Him, "Yes, Lord; You know that I love You." He said to him, "Tend My lambs." **16** He said to him again a second time, "Simon, *son* of John, do you love Me?" He said to Him, "Yes, Lord; You know that I love You." He said to him, "Shepherd My sheep." **17** He said to him the third time, "Simon, *son* of John, do you love Me?" Peter was grieved because He said to him the third time, "Do you love Me?" And he said to Him, "Lord, You know all things; You know that I love You." Jesus said to him, "Tend My sheep.

18 Truly, truly, I say to you, when you were younger, you used to gird yourself and walk wherever you wished; but when you grow old, you will stretch out your hands and someone else will gird you, and bring you where you do not wish to *go*." **19** Now this He said, signifying by what kind of death he would glorify God. And when He had spoken this, He said to him, "Follow Me!"

20 Peter, turning around, saw the disciple whom Jesus loved following *them*; the one who also had leaned back on His bosom at the supper and said, "Lord, who is the one who betrays You?" **21** So Peter seeing him said to Jesus, "Lord, and what about this man?" **22** Jesus said to him, "If I want him to remain until I come, what *is that* to you? You follow Me!" **23** Therefore this saying went out among the brethren that that disciple would not die; yet Jesus did not say to him that he would not die, but *only*, "If I want him to remain until I come, what *is that* to you?"

24 This is the disciple who is testifying to these things and wrote these things, and we know that his testimony is true.

25 And there are also many other things which Jesus did, which if they were written in detail, I suppose that even the world itself would not contain the books that would be written.

What is the Good News?
Romans

The word "gospel" means "the good news". More specifically, the letter to the Romans explains that the gospel is the good news that we can have peace with God and power for living through Jesus Christ. Yet before we can receive the good news, we must understand that there is bad news as well. The bad news is that we cannot please God because we all have broken God's law in order to love and serve ourselves. Thankfully, God's good news is greater than our bad news.

Some people shy away from the book of Romans because they think it is too complex. What follows in this section is a letter the apostle Paul wrote to a very young Church that he had never visited. He wrote it to them so that they would be familiar with the foundational teachings of Christ and understand the basics of their relationship with him. If you run into any parts that are hard to understand, just skip over them for now and focus on the main ideas. I pray that the gospel taught in the book of Romans will lay a foundation of grace in your life so that you can live in the power of the Holy Spirit.

1 This letter is from Paul[bb], a slave of Christ Jesus, chosen by God to be an apostle and sent out to preach his Good News. [2] God promised this Good News long ago through his prophets in the holy Scriptures. [3] The Good News is about his Son. In his earthly life he was born into King David's family line, [4] and he was shown to be the Son of God when he was raised from the dead by the power of the Holy Spirit. He is Jesus Christ our Lord. [5] Through Christ, God has given us the privilege and authority as apostles to tell Gentiles everywhere what God has done for them, so that they will believe and obey him, bringing glory to his name.

[6] And you are included among those Gentiles who have been called to belong to Jesus Christ. [7] I am writing to all of you in Rome who are loved by God and are called to be his own holy people.

May God our Father and the Lord Jesus Christ give you grace and peace.

[8] Let me say first that I thank my God through Jesus Christ for all of you, because your faith in him is being talked about all over the world. [9] God knows how often I pray for you. Day and night I bring you and your needs in prayer to God, whom I serve with all my heart by spreading the Good News about his Son.

[10] One of the things I always pray for is the opportunity, God willing, to come at last to see you. [11] For I long to visit you so I can bring you some spiritual gift that will help you grow strong in the Lord. [12] When we get together, I want to encourage you in your faith, but I also want to be encouraged by yours.

[13] I want you to know, dear brothers and sisters, that I planned many times to visit you, but I was prevented until now. I want to work among you and see spiritual fruit, just as I have seen among

---

[bb] *Paul:* After Jesus died and rose again, his followers were persecuted by the Jewish authorities. One of the men who pursued the Christians came to believe in Jesus through a vivid encounter with Him. This man came to be known as the apostle Paul, perhaps the greatest missionary the world has ever known (apostle means "sent-out-one"). Paul and his companions travelled throughout the Roman Empire telling the good news of Jesus to anyone who would listen, whatever their racial, ethnic, or religious background.

other Gentiles.¹⁴ For I have a great sense of obligation to people in both the civilized world and the rest of the world, to the educated and uneducated alike.¹⁵ So I am eager to come to you in Rome, too, to preach the Good News.

¹⁶ For I am not ashamed of this Good News about Christ. It is the power of God at work, saving everyone who believes—the Jew first and also the Gentile. ¹⁷ This Good News tells us how God makes us right in his sight. This is accomplished from start to finish by faith. As the Scriptures say, "It is through faith that a righteous person has life[cc]."

☛ Guidepost 11
The Good News Reveals that All People Are Under God's Wrath

¹⁸ For the wrath of God is revealed from heaven against all ungodliness and unrighteousness of men, who by their unrighteousness suppress the truth. ¹⁹ For what can be known about God is plain to them, because God has shown it to them. ²⁰ For his invisible attributes, namely, his eternal power and divine nature, have been clearly perceived, ever since the creation of the world, in the things that have been made. So they are without excuse. ²¹ For although they knew God, they did not honor him as God or give thanks to him, but they became futile in their thinking, and their foolish hearts were darkened. ²² Claiming to be wise, they became fools, ²³ and exchanged the glory of the immortal God for images resembling mortal man and birds and animals and creeping things.

[cc] *It is through faith that a righteous person has life:* The entire book of Romans can be viewed as a sermon on this one verse from the Old Testament book of Habakuk. First, we learn *who* is righteous; sadly, not one of us is righteous, for we have all pursued our own gain rather than God's glory. Therefore, we must learn how we can *become* righteous. The answer is that we can only become righteous through faith in Jesus Christ. Finally, we learn how we are to *live* by faith.

²⁴ Therefore God gave them up in the lusts of their hearts to impurity, to the dishonoring of their bodies among themselves, ²⁵ because they exchanged the truth about God for a lie and worshiped and served the creature rather than the Creator, who is blessed forever! Amen.

²⁶ For this reason God gave them up to dishonorable passions. For their women exchanged natural relations for those that are contrary to nature; ²⁷ and the men likewise gave up natural relations with women and were consumed with passion for one another, men committing shameless acts with men and receiving in themselves the due penalty for their error.

²⁸ And since they did not see fit to acknowledge God, God gave them up to a debased mind to do what ought not to be done. ²⁹ They were filled with all manner of unrighteousness, evil, covetousness, malice. They are full of envy, murder, strife, deceit, maliciousness. They are gossips,³⁰ slanderers, haters of God, insolent, haughty, boastful, inventors of evil, disobedient to parents, ³¹ foolish, faithless, heartless, ruthless.³² Though they know God's righteous decree that those who practice such things deserve to die, they not only do them but give approval to those who practice them.

2 Therefore you have no excuse, O man, every one of you who judges. For in passing judgment on another you condemn yourself, because you, the judge, practice the very same things. ² We know that the judgment of God rightly falls on those who practice such things. ³ Do you suppose, O man—you who judge those who practice such things and yet do them yourself—that you will escape the judgment of God? ⁴ Or do you presume on the riches of his kindness and forbearance and patience, not knowing that God's kindness is meant to lead you to repentance? ⁵ But because of your hard and impenitent heart you are storing up wrath for yourself on the day of wrath when God's righteous judgment will be revealed.

⁶ He will render to each one according to his works:

☞ Discussion 11
What does this guidepost teach about the Good News?

The gospel is "good news". But to understand how good the good news is, we must hear some bad news first. The bad news is all mankind is under God's wrath. Merriam-Webster defines wrath as "retributory punishment for an offense or a crime". What is our crime? That though we are graciously given life and all things by God, we don't honor Him or live lives of gratitude, but instead spend our lives seeking our fulfillment, security, and happiness in other things. This rebellious self-serving nature of ours results in our committing all kinds of wickedness. God does not force obedience; three times in these verses it says that God "gave them up" to do all that our wicked hearts could conceive. In committing treason against God, we have cut ourselves off from the source of life and light. Ultimately, if we remain under God's wrath, we will die forever separated from Him, at which time we will receive the full punishment for our rebellion. Remember Jesus' words: that He did not come into the world to condemn the world, for the world was already condemned.

Notice that it is not only the wicked who are called out as being under God's wrath. It is easy to read this passage and see only the sins of others. However, in the final paragraph Paul points directly at those who, in their pride and with a hard heart toward God, judge and accuse others. Paul calls out religious people who had the Scriptures but still did not obey them. There are two major ways in which mankind turns away from God. Some of us turn away from God in immorality and irreligion. Others turn away from God in legalistic religion. Yet we are all the same, for we all turn away, and we all remain under God's wrath.

- *When someone commits an offense against us, we often become bitter and want immediate justice. Why do you think that God instead gives us over to follow our desires? What does this say about God's character?*
- *Consider your own life. Would you say that it has been your tendency to follow your own desires toward irreligion or toward legalistic religion? Can you see how both paths are a turning away from God?*

---

7 He will give eternal life to those who keep on doing good, seeking after the glory and honor and immortality that God offers. 8 But he will pour out his anger and wrath on those who live for themselves, who refuse to obey the truth and instead live lives of wickedness. 9 There will be trouble and calamity for everyone who keeps on doing what is evil—for the Jew first and also for the Gentile. 10 But there will be glory and honor and peace from God for all who do good—for the Jew first and also for the Gentile. 11 For God does not show favoritism.

12 When the Gentiles sin, they will be destroyed, even though they never had God's written law. And the Jews, who do have God's law[dd], will be judged by that law when they fail to obey it. 13 For merely listening to the law doesn't make us right with God. It is obeying the law that makes us right in his sight. 14 Even Gentiles, who do not have God's written law, show that they know his law when they instinctively obey it, even without having heard it. 15 They demonstrate that God's law is written in their hearts, for their own conscience and thoughts either accuse them or tell them they are doing right. 16 And this is the message I proclaim—that the day is coming when God, through Christ Jesus, will judge everyone's secret life.

---

dd *The law.* The Old Testament scriptures. In the discussion that follows, Paul contrasts the plight of the Gentiles (non-Jewish peoples) who did not have the scriptures and thus sinned in ignorance with the Jews, who had the scriptures yet still sinned

17 You who call yourselves Jews are relying on God's law, and you boast about your special relationship with him. 18 You know what he wants; you know what is right because you have been taught his law. 19 You are convinced that you are a guide for the blind and a light for people who are lost in darkness. 20 You think you can instruct the ignorant and teach children the ways of God. For you are certain that God's law gives you complete knowledge and truth.

21 Well then, if you teach others, why don't you teach yourself? You tell others not to steal, but do you steal? 22 You say it is wrong to commit adultery, but do you commit adultery? You condemn idolatry, but do you use items stolen from pagan temples? 23 You are so proud of knowing the law, but you dishonor God by breaking it. 24 No wonder the Scriptures say, "The Gentiles blaspheme the name of God because of you."

25 The Jewish ceremony of circumcision has value only if you obey God's law. But if you don't obey God's law, you are no better off than an uncircumcised Gentile. 26 And if the Gentiles obey God's law, won't God declare them to be his own people? 27 In fact, uncircumcised Gentiles who keep God's law will condemn you Jews who are circumcised and possess God's law but don't obey it.

28 For you are not a true Jew just because you were born of Jewish parents or because you have gone through the ceremony of circumcision. 29 No, a true Jew is one whose heart is right with God. And true circumcision is not merely obeying the letter of the law; rather, it is a change of heart produced by the Spirit. And a person with a changed heart seeks praise from God, not from people.

3 Then what's the advantage of being a Jew? Is there any value in the ceremony of circumcision? 2 Yes, there are great benefits! First of all, the Jews were entrusted with the whole revelation of God.

3 True, some of them were unfaithful; but just because they were unfaithful, does that mean God will be unfaithful? 4 Of course not! Even if everyone else is a liar, God is true. As the Scriptures say about him,

"You will be proved right in what you say, and you will win your case in court."

⁵ "But," some might say, "our sinfulness serves a good purpose, for it helps people see how righteous God is. Isn't it unfair, then, for him to punish us?" (This is merely a human point of view.) ⁶ Of course not! If God were not entirely fair, how would he be qualified to judge the world?⁷ "But," someone might still argue, "how can God condemn me as a sinner if my dishonesty highlights his truthfulness and brings him more glory?" ⁸ And some people even slander us by claiming that we say, "The more we sin, the better it is!" Those who say such things deserve to be condemned.

⁹ Well then, should we conclude that we Jews are better than others? No, not at all, for we have already shown that all people, whether Jews or Gentiles, are under the power of sin. ¹⁰ As the Scriptures say,

"No one is righteous— not even one. ¹¹ No one is truly wise; no one is seeking God.¹² All have turned away; all have become useless. No one does good, not a single one."

¹³ "Their talk is foul, like the stench from an open grave. Their tongues are filled with lies."

"Snake venom drips from their lips."

¹⁴ "Their mouths are full of cursing and bitterness."

¹⁵ "They rush to commit murder. ¹⁶ Destruction and misery always follow them. ¹⁷ They don't know where to find peace."

¹⁸ "They have no fear of God at all."

¹⁹ Obviously, the law applies to those to whom it was given, for its purpose is to keep people from having excuses, and to show that the entire world is guilty before God. ²⁰ For no one can ever be made right with God by doing what the law commands. The law simply shows us how sinful we are.

✝ Guidepost 12
The Good News Reveals that Sinners Can Be Justified by Faith in Jesus Christ

21 But now the righteousness of God has been manifested apart from the law, although the Law and the Prophets bear witness to it— 22 the righteousness of God through faith in Jesus Christ for all who believe. For there is no distinction: 23 for all have sinned and fall short of the glory of God, 24 and are justified by his grace as a gift, through the redemption that is in Christ Jesus, 25 whom God put forward as a propitiation by his blood, to be received by faith. This was to show God's righteousness, because in his divine forbearance he had passed over former sins. 26 It was to show his righteousness at the present time, so that he might be just and the justifier of the one who has faith in Jesus.

27 Then what becomes of our boasting? It is excluded. By what kind of law? By a law of works? No, but by the law of faith. 28 For we hold that one is justified by faith apart from works of the law. 29 Or is God the God of Jews only? Is he not the God of Gentiles also? Yes, of Gentiles also, 30 since God is one—who will justify the circumcised by faith and the uncircumcised through faith.

✝ Discussion 12
What does this guidepost teach about the Good News?

After so much bad news we finally get to the good. Just as the gospel reveals God's wrath against our sin, so now it reveals how

---

we can again come into God's presence and avoid His wrath. The question before us is one of the most important questions in the Bible: how can a holy God have a relationship with those who have offended His holiness through their sin and rebellion? God's holiness and sense of justice demands that He judge sin; He cannot simply allow the guilty to go unpunished. However, His love compels Him to find a means to save us from His wrath. You see the problem? How can God be both just and yet still justify sinners (declare them to be innocent)?

As we have seen, our sin offended God's holiness, and justice demands that we be punished. Enter Jesus. The gospel declares that sinners can be redeemed (bought back) through Jesus Christ. How did God buy us back? By putting forward His own Son pay the penalty for our sins.

God sent His own Son into the world to live a perfect life–the life that none of us have lived. Jesus alone, out of all who have ever lived, did not offend the holiness of God and therefore, Jesus alone stands before God perfectly innocent, not deserving of death. Yet as we have seen in the Book of John, Jesus willingly gave up His own life for us. He stood in our place, and suffered punishment on our behalf so that we could be spared God's wrath and be declared innocent. Why did He do this? In His own words, "Because God so loved the world". Only through Jesus could God both punish our sin and pardon us at the same time.

God's redemption of us is a gift. We do not deserve it and cannot earn it, but can only receive it. How do we receive God's gift? Through faith. When we turn from our ways and trust in what Christ has done for us, God applies the propitiating work of Jesus to us and receives us back as His own children. This is good news.

- *Most religions of the world teach some form of self-justification. As long as we pray correctly, or give enough, or perform religious ceremonies, then God may pardon us. How is the Christian faith different?*
- *Have you come to place in your life in which you are willing to turn from your previous way of life to follow Jesus Christ by faith and be saved? If not, what is still holding you back from trusting in Him? If you are ready to follow Christ, you can begin a relationship with Him right now. See Appendix 1.*

---

[31] Well then, if we emphasize faith, does this mean that we can forget about the law? Of course not! In fact, only when we have faith do we truly fulfill the law.

4 Abraham[ee] was, humanly speaking, the founder of our Jewish nation. What did he discover about being made right with God? [2] If his good deeds had made him acceptable to God, he would have had something to boast about. But that was not God's way. [3] For the Scriptures tell us, "Abraham believed God, and God counted him as righteous because of his faith."

[4] When people work, their wages are not a gift, but something they have earned. [5] But people are counted as righteous, not because of

---

[ee] *Abraham:* Centuries before Moses and the creation of the nation of Israel, God called a man named Abram (later renamed Abraham) out of his homeland near modern-day Iran to be his vessel through whom He would bless the world. Though Abraham and his wife Sarah were childless, God promised Abraham that he would be the father of many nations, that God would bless his descendants with a new land that God would show to him, and that through him and his descendants the entire world would be blessed. Abraham believed God and followed him by faith, and was thus justified through his faith in God's promise. Later, God instructed Abraham and his sons to be circumcised, the sign of participation in the promises of God that the Jews keep to this day in accordance to the law of Moses. Paul's point in this section is that Abraham was justified by faith before receiving circumcision, proving that it is not by keeping the law that one is justified, but by faith alone. Abraham is thus the father of all who believe, both Jews and Greeks.

their work, but because of their faith in God who forgives sinners. ⁶ David also spoke of this when he described the happiness of those who are declared righteous without working for it:

⁷ "Oh, what joy for those whose disobedience is forgiven, whose sins are put out of sight. ⁸ Yes, what joy for those whose record the LORD has cleared of sin."

⁹ Now, is this blessing only for the Jews, or is it also for uncircumcised Gentiles? Well, we have been saying that Abraham was counted as righteous by God because of his faith. ¹⁰ But how did this happen? Was he counted as righteous only after he was circumcised, or was it before he was circumcised? Clearly, God accepted Abraham before he was circumcised!

¹¹ Circumcision was a sign that Abraham already had faith and that God had already accepted him and declared him to be righteous—even before he was circumcised. So Abraham is the spiritual father of those who have faith but have not been circumcised. They are counted as righteous because of their faith. ¹² And Abraham is also the spiritual father of those who have been circumcised, but only if they have the same kind of faith Abraham had before he was circumcised.

¹³ Clearly, God's promise to give the whole earth to Abraham and his descendants was based not on his obedience to God's law, but on a right relationship with God that comes by faith. ¹⁴ If God's promise is only for those who obey the law, then faith is not necessary and the promise is pointless. ¹⁵ For the law always brings punishment on those who try to obey it. (The only way to avoid breaking the law is to have no law to break!)

¹⁶ So the promise is received by faith. It is given as a free gift. And we are all certain to receive it, whether or not we live according to the law of Moses, if we have faith like Abraham's. For Abraham is the father of all who believe. ¹⁷ That is what the Scriptures mean when God told him, "I have made you the father of many nations." This happened because Abraham believed in the God who brings the dead back to life and who creates new things out of nothing.

[18] Even when there was no reason for hope, Abraham kept hoping—believing that he would become the father of many nations. For God had said to him, "That's how many descendants you will have!" [19] And Abraham's faith did not weaken, even though, at about 100 years of age, he figured his body was as good as dead—and so was Sarah's womb.

[20] Abraham never wavered in believing God's promise. In fact, his faith grew stronger, and in this he brought glory to God. [21] He was fully convinced that God is able to do whatever he promises. [22] And because of Abraham's faith, God counted him as righteous. [23] And when God counted him as righteous, it wasn't just for Abraham's benefit. It was recorded [24] for our benefit, too, assuring us that God will also count us as righteous if we believe in him, the one who raised Jesus our Lord from the dead. [25] He was handed over to die because of our sins, and he was raised to life to make us right with God.

5 Therefore, since we have been made right in God's sight by faith, we have peace with God because of what Jesus Christ our Lord has done for us. [2] Because of our faith, Christ has brought us into this place of undeserved privilege where we now stand, and we confidently and joyfully look forward to sharing God's glory.

[3] We can rejoice, too, when we run into problems and trials, for we know that they help us develop endurance. [4] And endurance develops strength of character, and character strengthens our confident hope of salvation. [5] And this hope will not lead to disappointment. For we know how dearly God loves us, because he has given us the Holy Spirit to fill our hearts with his love.

[6] When we were utterly helpless, Christ came at just the right time and died for us sinners. [7] Now, most people would not be willing to die for an upright person, though someone might perhaps be willing to die for a person who is especially good. [8] But God showed his great love for us by sending Christ to die for us while we were still sinners. [9] And since we have been made right in God's sight by the blood of Christ, he will certainly save us from God's condemnation. [10] For

since our friendship with God was restored by the death of his Son while we were still his enemies, we will certainly be saved through the life of his Son. [11] So now we can rejoice in our wonderful new relationship with God[ff] because our Lord Jesus Christ has made us friends of God.

[12] When Adam sinned, sin entered the world. Adam's sin brought death, so death spread to everyone, for everyone sinned. [13] Yes, people sinned even before the law was given. But it was not counted as sin because there was not yet any law to break. [14] Still, everyone died—from the time of Adam to the time of Moses—even those who did not disobey an explicit commandment of God, as Adam did. Now Adam is a symbol, a representation of Christ, who was yet to come. [15] But there is a great difference between Adam's sin and God's gracious gift. For the sin of this one man, Adam, brought death to many. But even greater is God's wonderful grace and his gift of forgiveness to many through this other man, Jesus Christ. [16] And the result of God's gracious gift is very different from the result of that one man's sin. For Adam's sin led to condemnation, but God's free gift leads to our being made right with God, even though we are guilty of many sins. [17] For the sin of this one man, Adam, caused death to rule over many. But even greater is God's wonderful grace and his gift of righteousness, for all who receive it will live in triumph over sin and death through this one man, Jesus Christ.

[18] Yes, Adam's one sin brings condemnation for everyone, but Christ's one act of righteousness brings a right relationship with God and new life for everyone. [19] Because one person disobeyed God, many became sinners. But because one other person obeyed God, many will be made righteous.

[20] God's law was given so that all people could see how sinful they were. But as people sinned more and more, God's wonderful grace

---

[ff] *Our wonderful new relationship with God*: The point of this entire passage is that God has done much more for us in Christ than simply forgiving our sin. We have also obtained access into his grace so that we can live a new life in Christ through the power of His Holy Spirit

became more abundant. ²¹ So just as sin ruled over all people and brought them to death, now God's wonderful grace rules instead, giving us right standing with God and resulting in eternal life through Jesus Christ our Lord.

✝ Guidepost 13
The Good News Gives Us New Life in Christ

6 What shall we say then? Are we to continue in sin that grace may abound? ² By no means! How can we who died to sin still live in it? ³ Do you not know that all of us who have been baptized into Christ Jesus were baptized into his death? ⁴ We were buried therefore with him by baptism into death, in order that, just as Christ was raised from the dead by the glory of the Father, we too might walk in newness of life.

⁵ For if we have been united with him in a death like his, we shall certainly be united with him in a resurrection like his. ⁶ We know that our old self was crucified with him in order that the body of sin might be brought to nothing, so that we would no longer be enslaved to sin. ⁷ For one who has died has been set free from sin. ⁸ Now if we have died with Christ, we believe that we will also live with him. ⁹ We know that Christ, being raised from the dead, will never die again; death no longer has dominion over him. ¹⁰ For the death he died he died to sin, once for all, but the life he lives he lives to God. ¹¹ So you also must consider yourselves dead to sin and alive to God in Christ Jesus.

¹² Let not sin therefore reign in your mortal body, to make you obey its passions. ¹³ Do not present your members to sin as instruments for unrighteousness, but present yourselves to God as those who have been brought from death to life, and your members to God as instruments for righteousness. ¹⁴ For sin will have no dominion over you, since you are not under law but under grace.

15 What then? Are we to sin because we are not under law but under grace? By no means! 16 Do you not know that if you present yourselves to anyone as obedient slaves, you are slaves of the one whom you obey, either of sin, which leads to death, or of obedience, which leads to righteousness? 17 But thanks be to God, that you who were once slaves of sin have become obedient from the heart to the standard of teaching to which you were committed, 18 and, having been set free from sin, have become slaves of righteousness. 19 I am speaking in human terms, because of your natural limitations. For just as you once presented your members as slaves to impurity and to lawlessness leading to more lawlessness, so now present your members as slaves to righteousness leading to sanctification.

20 For when you were slaves of sin, you were free in regard to righteousness. 21 But what fruit were you getting at that time from the things of which you are now ashamed? For the end of those things is death. 22 But now that you have been set free from sin and have become slaves of God, the fruit you get leads to sanctification and its end, eternal life. 23 For the wages of sin is death, but the free gift of God is eternal life in Christ Jesus our Lord.

☛ Discussion 13
What does this guidepost teach about the Good News?

The gospel teaches that God has freely pardoned our sins by grace. Yet grace can be taken advantage of, for if there is forgiveness in Christ, what stops me from sinning even more?

The answer is that as followers of Jesus Christ we have been given new life in Him so that we no longer have to be enslaved by our old desires. Paul speaks of being baptized into Christ. Here, he is not talking about the physical act of being baptized with

---

water, but of the believer being totally immersed in the life, death and resurrection of Christ. This uniting of ourselves with Christ's death frees us from our old way of life, and our union with Christ in His resurrection empowers us to live a new life in Him. Sin no longer has the powerful hold over us it once had. As we grow in Christ, we will find that the sinful things we once loved have less appeal to us—we truly are dead to them.

Since we have died to sin and been given new life in Christ, we must continually remind ourselves of our new identity. This requires a change in our mindset. The reality is that we have been set free from sin, but we must *consider* ourselves dead to sin. The next few studies will clarify for us how we do that.

- *The good news of the gospel is not only that we have been forgiven of our sins, but that we are freed from sin's mastery over us. How must our mindset change to adjust to this reality?*
- *Have you come to place your faith in Jesus Christ as your Lord and Savior? What evidence is there in your life that your faith is genuine and that you have truly been given new life in Christ?*
- *Are you ready to publicly identify yourself as a follower of Jesus Christ? What steps would you need to take to do so?*

7 Now, dear brothers and sisters—you who are familiar with the law^{gg}—don't you know that the law applies only while a person is living? ² For example, when a woman marries, the law binds her to her husband as long as he is alive. But if he dies, the laws of marriage no longer apply to her. ³ So while her husband is alive, she would be committing adultery if she married another man. But if her husband

gg *familiar with the law.* While Paul is specifically referring to the law of Moses, at times in this section it seems that he is broadening his definition to include any rule-based approach to God.

dies, she is free from that law and does not commit adultery when she remarries.

4 So, my dear brothers and sisters, this is the point: You died to the power of the law when you died with Christ. And now you are united with the one who was raised from the dead. As a result, we can produce a harvest of good deeds for God. 5 When we were controlled by our old nature, sinful desires were at work within us, and the law aroused these evil desires[hh] that produced a harvest of sinful deeds, resulting in death. 6 But now we have been released from the law, for we died to it and are no longer captive to its power. Now we can serve God, not in the old way of obeying the letter of the law, but in the new way of living in the Spirit[ii].

7 Well then, am I suggesting that the law of God is sinful? Of course not! In fact, it was the law that showed me my sin. I would never have known that coveting is wrong if the law had not said, "You must not covet." 8 But sin used this command to arouse all kinds of covetous desires within me! If there were no law, sin would not have that power. 9 At one time I lived without understanding the law. But when I learned the command not to covet, for instance, the power of sin came to life, 10 and I died. So I discovered that the law's commands, which were supposed to bring life, brought spiritual death instead. 11 Sin took advantage of those commands and deceived me; it used the commands to kill me. 12 But still, the law itself is holy, and its commands are holy and right and good.

13 But how can that be? Did the law, which is good, cause my death? Of course not! Sin used what was good to bring about my

---

hh *the law aroused those evil desires*: Because of the sinful tendencies of our nature, we often respond to moral law with rebellion. When we are told we cannot have or do something, we desire it all the more.

ii *the new way of living in the Spirit*: In the extended discussion that follows, Paul describes this new way of life that is available to the Christian through the power of the Holy Spirit. The Christian life is not to be lived as though it were a set of rules to follow. It is an entirely new way of approaching God through the power He provides.

condemnation to death. So we can see how terrible sin really is. It uses God's good commands for its own evil purposes.

¹⁴ So the trouble is not with the law, for it is spiritual and good. The trouble is with me, for I am all too human, a slave to sin. ¹⁵ I don't really understand myself, for I want to do what is right, but I don't do it. Instead, I do what I hate. ¹⁶ But if I know that what I am doing is wrong, this shows that I agree that the law is good. ¹⁷ So I am not the one doing wrong; it is sin living in me that does it.

¹⁸ And I know that nothing good lives in me, that is, in my sinful nature. I want to do what is right, but I can't. ¹⁹ I want to do what is good, but I don't. I don't want to do what is wrong, but I do it anyway. ²⁰ But if I do what I don't want to do, I am not really the one doing wrong; it is sin living in me that does it.

✝ Guidepost 14
The Good News Gives Us a New Identity and Power for Living

²¹ So I find it to be a law that when I want to do right, evil lies close at hand. ²² For I delight in the law of God, in my inner being, ²³ but I see in my members another law waging war against the law of my mind and making me captive to the law of sin that dwells in my members. ²⁴ Wretched man that I am! Who will deliver me from this body of death? ²⁵ Thanks be to God through Jesus Christ our Lord! So then, I myself serve the law of God with my mind, but with my flesh I serve the law of sin.

8 There is therefore now no condemnation for those who are in Christ Jesus. ² For the law of the Spirit of life has set you free in Christ Jesus from the law of sin and death. ³ For God has done what the law, weakened by the flesh, could not do. By sending his own Son in the likeness of sinful flesh and for sin, he condemned sin in the flesh, ⁴ in order that the righteous requirement of the law might be fulfilled in us, who walk not according to the flesh but according to the Spirit. [5] For those who live according to the flesh set their minds on the things of the flesh, but those who live according to the Spirit set their minds on the things of the Spirit. [6] For to set the mind on the flesh is death, but to set the mind on the Spirit is life and peace. [7] For the mind that is set on the flesh is hostile to God, for it does not submit to God's law; indeed, it cannot. [8] Those who are in the flesh cannot please God.

[9] You, however, are not in the flesh but in the Spirit, if in fact the Spirit of God dwells in you. Anyone who does not have the Spirit of Christ does not belong to him. [10] But if Christ is in you, although the body is dead because of sin, the Spirit is life because of righteousness. [11] If the Spirit of him who raised Jesus from the dead dwells in you, he who raised Christ Jesus from the dead will also give life to your mortal bodies through his Spirit who dwells in you.

[12] So then, brothers, we are debtors, not to the flesh, to live according to the flesh. [13] For if you live according to the flesh you will die, but if by the Spirit you put to death the deeds of the body, you will live. [14] For all who are led by the Spirit of God are sons of God. [15] For you did not receive the spirit of slavery to fall back into fear, but you have received the Spirit of adoption as sons, by whom we cry, "Abba! Father!" [16] The Spirit himself bears witness with our spirit that we are children of God, [17] and if children, then heirs—heirs of God and fellow heirs with Christ, provided we suffer with him in order that we may also be glorified with him.

✝ Discussion 14
What does this guidepost teach about the Good News?

We often try to modify our own or others' behavior by drafting and enforcing rules. The problem is that no rule has ever supplied power for living; the only thing rules can do is to condemn us when we break them. An approach to God based on our own ability to keep His laws is doomed to failure.

This is why the gospel is such good news. The gospel gives us a new identity: no longer do we stand before God as condemned law–breakers. Instead, because of what Christ has done for us, we are fully accepted by God as His own children. We live out this new identity not by slavishly following a rule–based code, but by living our lives with our mind set on God's Holy Spirit.

The Holy Spirit is given as a gift to live within all who are true children of God. He reassures us that we indeed God's children and empowers us to live new lives. As we walk in constant communication with God through the Spirit, we are given the spiritual resources to live lives marked by love and peace.

- **How does a rule-based approach to life and faith only lead to frustration and condemnation?**
- **What does it mean to live out of your new identity as a child of God? How does this transform your approach to the Christian life? How does the Spirit work in your life to do what the law of God could never do?**
- **What does it mean "to set your mind on the Spirit is life and peace?" Have you received the Holy Spirit into your life? How would you know? Would you try to seek the Holy Spirit's guidance this week as you face various situations, praying for Him to guide you?**

🪧 Guidepost 15
The Good News Carries Us
Through Our Sufferings

18 For I consider that the sufferings of this present time are not worth comparing with the glory that is to be revealed to us. **19** For the creation waits with eager longing for the revealing of the sons of Godⁱⁱ. **20** For the creation was subjected to futility, not willingly, but because of him who subjected it, in hope **21** that the creation itself will be set free from its bondage to corruption and obtain the freedom of the glory of the children of God. **22** For we know that the whole creation has been groaning together in the pains of childbirth until now. **23** And not only the creation, but we ourselves, who have the firstfruits of the Spirit, groan inwardly as we wait eagerly for adoption as sons, the redemption of our bodies. **24** For in this hope we were saved. Now hope that is seen is not hope. For who hopes for what he sees? **25** But if we hope for what we do not see, we wait for it with patience.

26 Likewise the Spirit helps us in our weakness. For we do not know what to pray for as we ought, but the Spirit himself intercedes for us with groanings too deep for words. **27** And he who searches hearts knows what is the mind of the Spirit, because the Spirit intercedes for the saints according to the will of God. **28** And we know that for those who love God all things work together for good, for those who are called according to his purpose. **29** For those whom he foreknew he also predestined to be conformed to the image of his Son, in order that he might be the firstborn among many brothers. **30** And those whom he predestined he also called, and those whom he called he also justified, and those whom he justified he also glorified.

ⁱⁱ *the revealing of the sons of God:* The idea here is that one day, when Jesus brings all of the children of God into his glory, creation itself will be renewed and no longer subject to decay.

[31] What then shall we say to these things? If God is for us, who can be against us? [32] He who did not spare his own Son but gave him up for us all, how will he not also with him graciously give us all things? [33] Who shall bring any charge against God's elect? It is God who justifies. [34] Who is to condemn? Christ Jesus is the one who died—more than that, who was raised—who is at the right hand of God, who indeed is interceding for us. [35] Who shall separate us from the love of Christ? Shall tribulation, or distress, or persecution, or famine, or nakedness, or danger, or sword? [36] As it is written, "For your sake we are being killed all the day long; we are regarded as sheep to be slaughtered."

[37] No, in all these things we are more than conquerors through him who loved us. [38] For I am sure that neither death nor life, nor angels nor rulers, nor things present nor things to come, nor powers, [39] nor height nor depth, nor anything else in all creation, will be able to separate us from the love of God in Christ Jesus our Lord.

✝ Discussion 15
What does this guidepost teach about the Good News?

Suffering is an inevitable part of life, and though the Christian is not excused from it, our suffering is mediated through the perspective of faith. While some suffering is the result of the evil that we do to ourselves or one another, we also experience suffering as a result of living in a fallen world. Scripture teaches us that when mankind rebelled against God, creation itself was affected, so that we live in a world of suffering. While the Bible does not explicitly reveal why God subjected creation to futility, many Christian thinkers believe that one of the reasons God allows suffering is so that we do not set our heart on this

---

impermanent world but on God alone, the Unshakable One. C.S. Lewis famously observed that suffering is God's "megaphone to arouse a deaf world." It is often when we undergo the most severe trials that our eyes are fixed most desperately upon God. While the Bible does not fully address the reasons behind suffering, we are assured of three things in this passage.

1) God uses suffering to bring about something good. At the end of the day we trust that there is a purpose for our suffering. Remarkably, the Christian is able to rejoice in suffering, "knowing that suffering produces endurance, and endurance produces character, and character produces hope, and hope does not put us to shame, because God's love has been poured into our hearts through the Holy Spirit who has been given to us [Romans 5:3–5]."

2) God is present with us in our sufferings: Though there will be times when our suffering makes it difficult even to pray, God's Holy Spirit prays for us, present with us through all our trials.

3) Our sufferings are not an indicator that God does not love us. Many people going through trials may start doubting God's love and concern for them. God is not against you. If you are a Christian, nothing is able to separate you from the love of God. There will be a day when the glory of His love will eclipse every sorrow.

- *How is every form of suffering able to be traced back to human sin?*
- *How does the gospel teach us that God dealt with the problem of human sin?*
- *What does it mean to you that God himself has experienced suffering?*
- *What are some trials that you are currently going through? What do you think God might be saying to you through your suffering?*

9 With Christ as my witness, I speak with utter truthfulness. My conscience and the Holy Spirit confirm it. [2] My heart is filled with bitter sorrow and unending grief [3] for my people, my Jewish brothers and sisters. I would be willing to be forever cursed—cut off from Christ!—if that would save them. [4] They are the people of Israel, chosen to be God's adopted children. God revealed his glory to them. He made covenants with them and gave them his law. He gave them the privilege of worshiping him and receiving his wonderful promises. [5] Abraham, Isaac, and Jacob are their ancestors, and Christ himself was an Israelite as far as his human nature is concerned. And he is God, the one who rules over everything and is worthy of eternal praise! Amen.

[6] Well then, has God failed to fulfill his promise to Israel? [kk] No, for not all who are born into the nation of Israel are truly members of God's people! [7] Being descendants of Abraham doesn't make them truly Abraham's children. For the Scriptures say, "Isaac is the son through whom your descendants will be counted," though Abraham had other children, too. [8] This means that Abraham's physical descendants are not necessarily children of God. Only the children of the promise[ll] are considered to be Abraham's children. [9] For God had promised, "I will return about this time next year, and Sarah will have a son."

[kk] *Has God failed to fulfill his promise to Israel*: While it may appear at first as though Paul is abruptly changing the subject, this section of scripture is very related to the promises of the preceding section. The question being dealt with is: How can I be sure that God will keep His promise to never abandon me when it appears as though He failed to keep his promise to the Israelites, His chosen people? In short, is God a trustworthy God?

[ll] *children of the promise*:: Here we are introduced to some of the most important people in the family tree of the Jewish people. Abraham, the patriarch of this family, was promised particular blessings by God that would be passed on through his descendants. Paul's point in this passage is that even within the family tree of Abraham, there have always been selectivity on God's part regarding the transmission on of this promise. Out of Abraham's two sons, Isaac was chosen. Of Isaac and Rebecca's two son's, Jacob was chosen over Esau. Therefore, we should not be surprised that when Jesus came to fulfill the promise to Abraham, there was yet again another division within Israel.

¹⁰ This son was our ancestor Isaac. When he married Rebekah, she gave birth to twins. ¹¹ But before they were born, before they had done anything good or bad, she received a message from God. (This message shows that God chooses people according to his own purposes; ¹² he calls people, but not according to their good or bad works.) She was told, "Your older son will serve your younger son." ¹³ In the words of the Scriptures, "I loved Jacob, but I rejected Esau[mm]."

¹⁴ Are we saying, then, that God was unfair? Of course not! ¹⁵ For God said to Moses, "I will show mercy to anyone I choose, and I will show compassion to anyone I choose."

¹⁶ So it is God who decides to show mercy. We can neither choose it nor work for it.

¹⁷ For the Scriptures say that God told Pharaoh, "I have appointed you for the very purpose of displaying my power in you and to spread my fame throughout the earth." ¹⁸ So you see, God chooses to show mercy to some, and he chooses to harden the hearts of others so they refuse to listen.

¹⁹ Well then, you might say, "Why does God blame people for not responding? Haven't they simply done what he makes them do? [nn]"

²⁰ No, don't say that. Who are you, a mere human being, to argue with God? Should the thing that was created say to the one who created it, "Why have you made me like this?" ²¹ When a potter makes jars out of clay, doesn't he have a right to use the same lump of clay to make one jar for decoration and another to throw garbage into? ²² In the same way, even though God has the right to show his anger

---

mm *I loved Jacob, but I rejected Esau*. This seems to be an idiomatic phrase. God's 'love' of Jacob and rejecting of Esau are ways of describing in sharply contrasting terms God's selection of one over the other.

nn *Haven't they simply done what he makes them do?*: The question of how human responsibility coheres with God's sovereign choice in election is an in-house debate within Christianity. Theologians and philosophers have wrestled with this question for centuries, without resolution. No matter where one lands in the debate, however, Christians have always affirmed two truths that have set the boundaries for the debate: 1) God knows all things and superintends all things, and 2) Humans are responsible for their own moral choices.

and his power, he is very patient with those on whom his anger falls, who are destined for destruction. ²³ He does this to make the riches of his glory shine even brighter on those to whom he shows mercy, who were prepared in advance for glory. ²⁴ And we are among those whom he selected, both from the Jews and from the Gentiles.

²⁵ Concerning the Gentiles, God says in the prophecy of Hosea, "Those who were not my people, I will now call my people. And I will love those whom I did not love before." ²⁶ And, "Then, at the place where they were told, 'You are not my people,' there they will be called 'children of the living God.'"

²⁷ And concerning Israel, Isaiah the prophet cried out, "Though the people of Israel are as numerous as the sand of the seashore, only a remnant will be saved. ²⁸ For the LORD will carry out his sentence upon the earth quickly and with finality."

²⁹ And Isaiah said the same thing in another place: "If the LORD of Heaven's Armies had not spared a few of our children, we would have been wiped out like Sodom, destroyed like Gomorrah."

³⁰ What does all this mean? Even though the Gentiles were not trying to follow God's standards, they were made right with God. And it was by faith that this took place. ³¹ But the people of Israel, who tried so hard to get right with God by keeping the law, never succeeded. ³² Why not? Because they were trying to get right with God by keeping the law instead of by trusting in him. They stumbled over the great rock in their path. ³³ God warned them of this in the Scriptures when he said, "I am placing a stone in Jerusalem that makes people stumble, a rock that makes them fall. But anyone who trusts in him will never be disgraced."

10 Dear brothers and sisters, the longing of my heart and my prayer to God is for the people of Israel to be saved. ² I know what enthusiasm they have for God, but it is misdirected zeal. ³ For they don't understand God's way of making people right with himself. Refusing to accept God's way, they cling to their own way of getting right with God by trying to keep the law. ⁴ For Christ has already accomplished the purpose for which the law was given. As a result, all who believe in him are made right with God.

5 For Moses writes that the law's way of making a person right with God requires obedience to all of its commands. 6 But faith's way of getting right with God says, "Don't say in your heart, 'Who will go up to heaven?' (to bring Christ down to earth). 7 And don't say, 'Who will go down to the place of the dead?' (to bring Christ back to life again)." 8 In fact, it says, "The message is very close at hand; it is on your lips and in your heart."

And that message is the very message about faith that we preach: 9 If you openly declare that Jesus is Lord and believe in your heart that God raised him from the dead, you will be saved. 10 For it is by believing in your heart that you are made right with God, and it is by openly declaring your faith that you are saved. 11 As the Scriptures tell us, "Anyone who trusts in him will never be disgraced." 12 Jew and Gentile are the same in this respect. They have the same Lord, who gives generously to all who call on him. 13 For "Everyone who calls on the name of the LORD will be saved."

14 But how can they call on him to save them unless they believe in him? And how can they believe in him if they have never heard about him? And how can they hear about him unless someone tells them? 15 And how will anyone go and tell them without being sent? That is why the Scriptures say, "How beautiful are the feet of messengers who bring good news!"

16 But not everyone welcomes the Good News, for Isaiah the prophet said, "LORD, who has believed our message?" 17 So faith comes from hearing, that is, hearing the Good News about Christ. 18 But I ask, have the people of Israel actually heard the message? Yes, they have: "The message has gone throughout the earth, and the words to all the world."

19 But I ask, did the people of Israel really understand? Yes, they did, for even in the time of Moses, God said, "I will rouse your jealousy through people who are not even a nation. I will provoke your anger through the foolish Gentiles."

20 And later Isaiah spoke boldly for God, saying, "I was found by people who were not looking for me. I showed myself to those who were not asking for me."

21 But regarding Israel, God said, "All day long I opened my arms to them, but they were disobedient and rebellious."

🪧 Guidepost 16
The Good News is Grounded in a God Who Keeps His Promises

11 I ask, then, has God rejected his people? By no means! For I myself am an Israelite, a descendant of Abraham, a member of the tribe of Benjamin. **2** God has not rejected his people whom he foreknew. Do you not know what the Scripture says of Elijah, how he appeals to God against Israel? **3** "Lord, they have killed your prophets, they have demolished your altars, and I alone am left, and they seek my life." **4** But what is God's reply to him? "I have kept for myself seven thousand men who have not bowed the knee to Baal." **5** So too at the present time there is a remnant, chosen by grace. **6** But if it is by grace, it is no longer on the basis of works; otherwise grace would no longer be grace.

7 What then? Israel failed to obtain what it was seeking. The elect obtained it, but the rest were hardened, **8** as it is written, "God gave them a spirit of stupor, eyes that would not see and ears that would not hear, down to this very day."

9 And David says, "Let their table become a snare and a trap, a stumbling block and a retribution for them; **10** let their eyes be darkened so that they cannot see, and bend their backs forever."

11 So I ask, did they stumble in order that they might fall? By no means! Rather, through their trespass salvation has come to the Gentiles, so as to make Israel jealous. **12** Now if their trespass means riches for the world, and if their failure means riches for the Gentiles, how much more will their full inclusion mean!

[13] Now I am speaking to you Gentiles. Inasmuch then as I am an apostle to the Gentiles, I magnify my ministry [14] in order somehow to make my fellow Jews jealous, and thus save some of them. [15] For if their rejection means the reconciliation of the world, what will their acceptance mean but life from the dead? [16] If the dough offered as firstfruits is holy, so is the whole lump, and if the root is holy, so are the branches.

✝ Discussion 16
What does this guidepost teach about the Good News?

The question of God's character is a very important one. The Roman gods were known for their whimsy and capricious nature. They could change their minds or toy with humans. If they were not appeased, they would remove their favor and act out in vengeance. Is the Christian God of similar character? Can we trust God to follow through on His promises to His people?

The answer scripture gives to this question is a resounding yes. Taking Israel as a case study, Paul argues that God has always preserved a faithful remnant to keep His promises, even when the majority of the nation were led astray to worship other gods. Though most of the Jews rejected Jesus as Messiah, many did receive Him, including Paul himself, demonstrating that God had not fully rejected His people.

Moreover, God has used the fact that most of the Jews rejected His Messiah for good, for it was through their rejection of the gospel that the message of salvation was taken to the Gentiles. Yet Paul still prays for his people, that ultimately they will turn to Christ and be once again fully included and accepted in God's salvation.

- *This section of Scripture contains some concepts that might be difficult to understand or receive, such as God's election and hardening. Some people reject God because of something that does not seem fair to them. Are you able to trust God even when you don't understand all of His ways?*
- *What difference does it make in your Christian life to be assured that God is a God who keeps His promises made to His people?*
- *Paul is very personally committed to seeing the gospel of Christ accepted among his people. Think about your people group or ethnic background. How is God working among your people?*

¹⁷ But some of these branches from Abraham's tree—some of the people of Israel—have been broken off. And you Gentiles, who were branches from a wild olive tree, have been grafted in. So now you also receive the blessing God has promised Abraham and his children, sharing in the rich nourishment from the root of God's special olive tree. ¹⁸ But you must not brag about being grafted in to replace the branches that were broken off. You are just a branch, not the root.

¹⁹ "Well," you may say, "those branches were broken off to make room for me." ²⁰ Yes, but remember—those branches were broken off because they didn't believe in Christ, and you are there because you do believe. So don't think highly of yourself, but fear what could

happen. ²¹ For if God did not spare the original branches, he won't spare you either°°.

²² Notice how God is both kind and severe. He is severe toward those who disobeyed, but kind to you if you continue to trust in his kindness. But if you stop trusting, you also will be cut off. ²³ And if the people of Israel turn from their unbelief, they will be grafted in again, for God has the power to graft them back into the tree. ²⁴ You, by nature, were a branch cut from a wild olive tree. So if God was willing to do something contrary to nature by grafting you into his cultivated tree, he will be far more eager to graft the original branches back into the tree where they belong.

²⁵ I want you to understand this mystery, dear brothers and sisters, so that you will not feel proud about yourselves. Some of the people of Israel have hard hearts, but this will last only until the full number of Gentiles comes to Christ. ²⁶ And so all Israel will be saved. As the Scriptures say, "The one who rescues will come from Jerusalem, and he will turn Israel away from ungodliness. ²⁷ And this is my covenant with them, that I will take away their sins."

²⁸ Many of the people of Israel are now enemies of the Good News, and this benefits you Gentiles. Yet they are still the people he loves because he chose their ancestors Abraham, Isaac, and Jacob. ²⁹ For God's gifts and his call can never be withdrawn. ³⁰ Once, you Gentiles were rebels against God, but when the people of Israel rebelled against him, God was merciful to you instead. ³¹ Now they are the rebels, and God's mercy has come to you so that they, too, will share in God's mercy. ³² For God has imprisoned everyone in disobedience so he could have mercy on everyone.

³³ Oh, how great are God's riches and wisdom and knowledge! How impossible it is for us to understand his decisions and his ways! ³⁴ For who can know the LORD's thoughts? Who knows enough to

---

°° *For if God did not spare the orginal branches, he won't spare you either:* God will save no one on the basis of their ethnicity or people group, but only those who come to faith in His Son

give him advice? ³⁵ And who has given him so much   that he needs to pay it back?

³⁶ For everything comes from him and exists by his power and is intended for his glory. All glory to him forever! Amen.

☛ Guidepost 17
The Good News Calls Us to an Appropriate Response

12 I appeal to you therefore, brothers, by the mercies of God, to present your bodies as a living sacrifice, holy and acceptable to God, which is your spiritual worship. ² Do not be conformed to this world, but be transformed by the renewal of your mind, that by testing you may discern what is the will of God, what is good and acceptable and perfect.

³ For by the grace given to me I say to everyone among you not to think of himself more highly than he ought to think, but to think with sober judgment, each according to the measure of faith that God has assigned. ⁴ For as in one body we have many members, and the members do not all have the same function, ⁵ so we, though many, are one body in Christ, and individually members one of another. ⁶ Having gifts that differ according to the grace given to us, let us use them: if prophecy, in proportion to our faith; ⁷ if service, in our serving; the one who teaches, in his teaching; ⁸ the one who exhorts, in his exhortation; the one who contributes, in generosity; the one who leads, with zeal; the one who does acts of mercy, with cheerfulness.

⁹ Let love be genuine. Abhor what is evil; hold fast to what is good.¹⁰ Love one another with brotherly affection. Outdo one another in showing honor. ¹¹ Do not be slothful in zeal, be fervent in spirit, serve the Lord. ¹² Rejoice in hope, be patient in tribulation, be

constant in prayer. [13] Contribute to the needs of the saints and seek to show hospitality.

[14] Bless those who persecute you; bless and do not curse them. [15] Rejoice with those who rejoice, weep with those who weep. [16] Live in harmony with one another. Do not be haughty, but associate with the lowly. Never be wise in your own sight. [17] Repay no one evil for evil, but give thought to do what is honorable in the sight of all. [18] If possible, so far as it depends on you, live peaceably with all. [19] Beloved, never avenge yourselves, but leave it to the wrath of God, for it is written, "Vengeance is mine, I will repay, says the Lord." [20] To the contrary, "if your enemy is hungry, feed him; if he is thirsty, give him something to drink; for by so doing you will heap burning coals on his head." [21] Do not be overcome by evil, but overcome evil with good.

✝ Discussion 17
What does this guidepost teach about the Good News?

This passage is a turning point in the letter to the Romans. Up until now, the letter has been primarily theoretical and theological, detailing the immeasurable mercies of God. The rest of the letter turns personal and practical: turning us toward the sort of life that the mercies of God direct us to live.

Every invitation calls for an appropriate response. If I am invited to a person's home for dinner, I could respond by rejecting or accepting the invitation. Even in accepting the invitation, an appropriate response is needed. It would be inappropriate to try to pay the host for dinner, or to show up hours late, drunk, or underdressed. Our appropriate response to the invitation does not take away from the graciousness of the invitation itself. As we

---

have seen in the case of our salvation, the invitation is entirely undeserved. So what response is appropriate?

The appropriate response that the gospel calls us to is to turn our lives over to God as an act of worship. This is a measured, considered response to Jesus Christ, in which we recognize his Lordship over us. Just as Jesus acted as a priest, presenting Himself as a sacrificial lamb on our behalf, we now are called to act as priests in response, presenting ourselves to God to be used by Him–not in death, but in life.

When we come to Christ by presenting ourselves to Him in this way, God begins to transform us. Up until this point, all of us have more or less followed the conventional wisdom of the world around us–either that of the broader culture or of a particular sub-culture with which we identify. In coming to Christ, however, we find that much of the conventional wisdom we built our lives upon has led us away from God. Thus, much of our old ways of thinking must be reappraised in light of God and his revelation to us. As we continue to read, study, and obey the Scriptures with a humble heart, the Holy Spirit will transform us, producing more and more confidence in God and His will for us.

For example, the conventional wisdom of this world might be to avoid one's enemies. In some situations, we would even be tempted to retaliate against our enemies. Yet the gospel teaches us to love, bless and even feed our enemies, for we can trust God to judge our enemies with severe justice. To be honest, the first time I bless someone who seeks my pain, I may not fully trust the Lord's will, yet as I test the Lord's ways I find that His ways are truly good, acceptable and perfect.

- *Do you feel a life of love will bring you more happiness than a life of selfishness?*
- *Have you prayerfully and thoughtfully presented your life to God as a response to His mercies? If not, what is still holding you back? Would you do so now? If so, please see Appendix 1*
- *Will you commit yourself to continue studying the Scripture with a humble attitude, open to the Holy Spirit's work of transformation in your life?*
- *Notice that this passage speaks of using our gifts to love and serve other members of the body of Christ. The Christian life is not meant to be lived alone. If you are not involved in a community of other believers, can you see the benefit of finding a local church that loves Jesus and humbly seeks to follow the Scriptures?*

13 Everyone must submit to governing authorities. For all authority comes from God, and those in positions of authority have been placed there by God. [2] So anyone who rebels against authority is rebelling against what God has instituted, and they will be punished. [3] For the authorities do not strike fear in people who are doing right, but in those who are doing wrong. Would you like to live without fear of the authorities? Do what is right, and they will honor you. [4] The authorities are God's servants, sent for your good. But if you are doing wrong, of course you should be afraid, for they have the power to punish you. They are God's servants, sent for the very purpose of punishing those who do what is wrong. [5] So you must submit to them, not only to avoid punishment, but also to keep a clear conscience.

[6] Pay your taxes, too, for these same reasons. For government workers need to be paid. They are serving God in what they do. [7] Give to everyone what you owe them: Pay your taxes and government fees to those who collect them, and give respect and honor to those who are in authority.

⁸ Owe nothing to anyone—except for your obligation to love one another. If you love your neighbor, you will fulfill the requirements of God's law.⁹ For the commandments say, "You must not commit adultery. You must not murder. You must not steal. You must not covet." These—and other such commandments—are summed up in this one commandment: "Love your neighbor as yourself." ¹⁰ Love does no wrong to others, so love fulfills the requirements of God's law.

¹¹ This is all the more urgent, for you know how late it is; time is running out. Wake up, for our salvation is nearer now than when we first believed. ¹² The night is almost gone; the day of salvation will soon be here. So remove your dark deeds like dirty clothes, and put on the shining armor of right living. ¹³ Because we belong to the day, we must live decent lives for all to see. Don't participate in the darkness of wild parties and drunkenness, or in sexual promiscuity and immoral living, or in quarreling and jealousy. ¹⁴ Instead, clothe yourself with the presence of the Lord Jesus Christ. And don't let yourself think about ways to indulge your evil desires.

⛨ Guidepost 18
The Good News Makes Us More Tolerant and Joyful

14 As for the one who is weak in faith, welcome him, but not to quarrel over opinions. ² One person believes he may eat anything, while the weak person eats only vegetables. ³ Let not the one who eats despise the one who abstains, and let not the one who abstains pass judgment on the one who eats, for God has welcomed him. ⁴ Who are you to pass judgment on the servant of another? It is before his own master that he stands or falls. And he will be upheld, for the Lord is able to make him stand.

5 One person esteems one day as better than another, while another esteems all days alike. Each one should be fully convinced in his own mind. **6** The one who observes the day, observes it in honor of the Lord. The one who eats, eats in honor of the Lord, since he gives thanks to God, while the one who abstains, abstains in honor of the Lord and gives thanks to God. **7** For none of us lives to himself, and none of us dies to himself. **8** For if we live, we live to the Lord, and if we die, we die to the Lord. So then, whether we live or whether we die, we are the Lord's. **9** For to this end Christ died and lived again, that he might be Lord both of the dead and of the living.

10 Why do you pass judgment on your brother? Or you, why do you despise your brother? For we will all stand before the judgment seat of God; **11** for it is written, "As I live, says the Lord, every knee shall bow to me, and every tongue shall confess to God." **12** So then each of us will give an account of himself to God.

13 Therefore let us not pass judgment on one another any longer, but rather decide never to put a stumbling block or hindrance in the way of a brother. **14** I know and am persuaded in the Lord Jesus that nothing is unclean in itself, but it is unclean for anyone who thinks it unclean. **15** For if your brother is grieved by what you eat, you are no longer walking in love. By what you eat, do not destroy the one for whom Christ died. **16** So do not let what you regard as good be spoken of as evil. **17** For the kingdom of God is not a matter of eating and drinking but of righteousness and peace and joy in the Holy Spirit. **18** Whoever thus serves Christ is acceptable to God and approved by men. **19** So then let us pursue what makes for peace and for mutual upbuilding.

20 Do not, for the sake of food, destroy the work of God. Everything is indeed clean, but it is wrong for anyone to make another stumble by what he eats. **21** It is good not to eat meat or drink wine or do anything that causes your brother to stumble. **22** The faith that you have, keep between yourself and God. Blessed is the one who has no reason to pass judgment on himself for what he approves.

²³ But whoever has doubts is condemned if he eats, because the eating is not from faith. For whatever does not proceed from faith is sin.

15 We who are strong have an obligation to bear with the failings of the weak, and not to please ourselves. ² Let each of us please his neighbor for his good, to build him up. ³ For Christ did not please himself, but as it is written, "The reproaches of those who reproached you fell on me."⁴ For whatever was written in former days was written for our instruction, that through endurance and through the encouragement of the Scriptures we might have hope. ⁵ May the God of endurance and encouragement grant you to live in such harmony with one another, in accord with Christ Jesus, ⁶ that together you may with one voice glorify the God and Father of our Lord Jesus Christ.

✝ Discussion 18
What does this guidepost teach about the Good News?

Religious people have a well-earned reputation for being judgmental. The good news of Jesus Christ, however, teaches us to pursue peace with others even when we disagree over how exactly we are to live out our faith.

It is necessary for Christians to form their own convictions according to principles found in the scriptures. However, since the Bible does not directly speak to every situation we may face, not every Christian will apply the teachings of scripture the same way. For example, a person who had a drinking problem before coming to Christ might believe that it is best to abstain from alcohol completely, while another Christian might not feel that total abstention is necessary for himself. The main concern in this passage is that while it is important for us to develop our own

---

convictions from God's word, we should live at peace with others as they live before God according to their own convictions. We trust that God is working in them for their holiness just as He is working in us for ours. This is the practical outworking of love to which the good news calls us.

It is true that religion often makes us joyless, judgmental jerks. The Holy Spirit, however, transforms us into people of righteousness, peace and joy. For just as we have found a peace and love in Christ, we pursue peace and extend the same type of love to others.

> *Why is it necessary for each Christian to develop their own lifestyle convictions? What role does the word of God and other Christians play in helping form those convictions?*
> *What are some sorts of lifestyle convictions that Christians may form different conviction about?*
> *What does it mean to welcome others in the faith who share different lifestyle convictions? What would that look like in your life?*

⁷ Therefore, accept each other just as Christ has accepted you so that God will be given glory. ⁸ Remember that Christ came as a servant to the Jews to show that God is true to the promises he made to their ancestors. ⁹ He also came so that the Gentiles might give glory to God for his mercies to them. That is what the psalmist meant when he wrote: "For this, I will praise you among the Gentiles; I will sing praises to your name."

¹⁰ And in another place it is written, "Rejoice with his people, you Gentiles."

¹¹ And yet again, "Praise the LORD, all you Gentiles. Praise him, all you people of the earth."

¹² And in another place Isaiah said, "The heir to David's throne will come, and he will rule over the Gentiles. They will place their hope on him."

¹³ I pray that God, the source of hope, will fill you completely with joy and peace because you trust in him. Then you will overflow with confident hope through the power of the Holy Spirit.

¹⁴ I am fully convinced, my dear brothers and sisters, that you are full of goodness. You know these things so well you can teach each other all about them. ¹⁵ Even so, I have been bold enough to write about some of these points, knowing that all you need is this reminder. For by God's grace, ¹⁶ I am a special messenger from Christ Jesus to you Gentiles. I bring you the Good News so that I might present you as an acceptable offering to God, made holy by the Holy Spirit. ¹⁷ So I have reason to be enthusiastic about all Christ Jesus has done through me in my service to God. ¹⁸ Yet I dare not boast about anything except what Christ has done through me, bringing the Gentiles to God by my message and by the way I worked among them. ¹⁹ They were convinced by the power of miraculous signs and wonders and by the power of God's Spirit. In this way, I have fully presented the Good News of Christ from Jerusalem all the way to Illyricum.

²⁰ My ambition has always been to preach the Good News where the name of Christ has never been heard, rather than where a church has already been started by someone else. ²¹ I have been following the plan spoken of in the Scriptures, where it says, "Those who have never been told about him will see, and those who have never heard of him will understand."

²² In fact, my visit to you has been delayed so long because I have been preaching in these places.

²³ But now I have finished my work in these regions, and after all these long years of waiting, I am eager to visit you. ²⁴ I am planning to go to Spain, and when I do, I will stop off in Rome. And after I have enjoyed your fellowship for a little while, you can provide for my journey.

25 But before I come, I must go to Jerusalem to take a gift to the believers there. **26** For you see, the believers in Macedonia and Achaia have eagerly taken up an offering for the poor among the believers in Jerusalem. **27** They were glad to do this because they feel they owe a real debt to them. Since the Gentiles received the spiritual blessings of the Good News from the believers in Jerusalem, they feel the least they can do in return is to help them financially. **28** As soon as I have delivered this money and completed this good deed of theirs, I will come to see you on my way to Spain. **29** And I am sure that when I come, Christ will richly bless our time together.

30 Dear brothers and sisters, I urge you in the name of our Lord Jesus Christ to join in my struggle by praying to God for me. Do this because of your love for me, given to you by the Holy Spirit. **31** Pray that I will be rescued from those in Judea who refuse to obey God. Pray also that the believers there will be willing to accept the donation I am taking to Jerusalem. **32** Then, by the will of God, I will be able to come to you with a joyful heart, and we will be an encouragement to each other.

33 And now may God, who gives us his peace, be with you all. Amen

16 I commend to you our sister Phoebe, who is a deacon in the church in Cenchrea. **2** Welcome her in the Lord as one who is worthy of honor among God's people. Help her in whatever she needs, for she has been helpful to many, and especially to me.

3 Give my greetings to Priscilla and Aquila, my co-workers in the ministry of Christ Jesus. **4** In fact, they once risked their lives for me. I am thankful to them, and so are all the Gentile churches. **5** Also give my greetings to the church that meets in their home.

Greet my dear friend Epenetus. He was the first person from the province of Asia to become a follower of Christ. **6** Give my greetings to Mary, who has worked so hard for your benefit. **7** Greet Andronicus and Junia, my fellow Jews, who were in prison with me. They are highly respected among the apostles and became followers of Christ before I did. [8] Greet Ampliatus, my dear friend in the Lord. [9] Greet Urbanus, our co-worker in Christ, and my dear friend Stachys.

[10] Greet Apelles, a good man whom Christ approves. And give my greetings to the believers from the household of Aristobulus. [11] Greet Herodion, my fellow Jew. Greet the Lord's people from the household of Narcissus. [12] Give my greetings to Tryphena and Tryphosa, the Lord's workers, and to dear Persis, who has worked so hard for the Lord. [13] Greet Rufus, whom the Lord picked out to be his very own; and also his dear mother, who has been a mother to me.

[14] Give my greetings to Asyncritus, Phlegon, Hermes, Patrobas, Hermas, and the brothers and sisters who meet with them. [15] Give my greetings to Philologus, Julia, Nereus and his sister, and to Olympas and all the believers who meet with them. [16] Greet each other with a sacred kiss. All the churches of Christ send you their greetings.

[17] And now I make one more appeal, my dear brothers and sisters. Watch out for people who cause divisions and upset people's faith by teaching things contrary to what you have been taught. Stay away from them. [18] Such people are not serving Christ our Lord; they are serving their own personal interests. By smooth talk and glowing words they deceive innocent people. [19] But everyone knows that you are obedient to the Lord. This makes me very happy. I want you to be wise in doing right and to stay innocent of any wrong. [20] The God of peace will soon crush Satan under your feet. May the grace of our Lord Jesus be with you.

[21] Timothy, my fellow worker, sends you his greetings, as do Lucius, Jason, and Sosipater, my fellow Jews.

[22] I, Tertius, the one writing this letter for Paul, send my greetings, too, as one of the Lord's followers.

[23] Gaius says hello to you. He is my host and also serves as host to the whole church. Erastus, the city treasurer, sends you his greetings, and so does our brother Quartus.

[25] Now all glory to God, who is able to make you strong, just as my Good News says. This message about Jesus Christ has revealed his plan for you Gentiles, a plan kept secret from the beginning of

time. ²⁶ But now as the prophets foretold and as the eternal God has commanded, this message is made known to all Gentiles everywhere, so that they too might believe and obey him. ²⁷ All glory to the only wise God, through Jesus Christ, forever. Amen.

What is Christian Freedom?
Galatians

The early Christians came from many different ethnic, social and economic backgrounds. One of the most divisive issues in the early church was that some Jewish Christians were putting pressure on non-Jewish ("Gentile") Christians to conform to their religious and cultural practices–in order to be a "good" Christian, everyone had to look and act exactly like them. The letter of Galatians is a scathing response to this mindset. Paul wrote that a message of ethnic and cultural superiority violates the gospel, for the gospel promises that Jesus saves all kinds of people.

Trying to earn salvation by conforming to the outward standards of others is called legalism and it is spiritually deadly because it denies that it is Jesus who saves us. While Christians are to respect the convictions of others, Christians are set free by the gospel of Christ to live according to the law of love through the power of the Spirit within them.

When you read each section, reflect upon what it teaches about Christian freedom. After you have answered for yourself, read the commentary and work through the questions.

✝ Guidepost 19
Freedom is Threatened by the
False Gospel of Legalism

1 Paul, an apostle–not from men nor through man, but through Jesus Christ and God the Father, who raised him from the dead– **2** and all the brothers who are with me,

To the churches of Galatia:

3 Grace to you and peace from God our Father and the Lord Jesus Christ, **4** who gave himself for our sins to deliver us from the present evil age, according to the will of our God and Father, **5** to whom be the glory forever and ever. Amen.

6 I am astonished that you are so quickly deserting him who called you in the grace of Christ and are turning to a different gospel– **7** not that there is another one, but there are some who trouble you and want to distort the gospel of Christ. **8** But even if we or an angel from heaven should preach to you a gospel contrary to the one we preached to you, let him be accursed. **9** As we have said before, so now I say again: If anyone is preaching to you a gospel contrary to the one you received, let him be accursed.

10 For am I now seeking the approval of man, or of God? Or am I trying to please man? If I were still trying to please man, I would not be a servant of Christ.

✝ Discussion 19
What does this guidepost teach about freedom in Christ?

Since the beginning of the Christian faith, false teachings have arisen under the guise of the gospel. We must be careful, therefore, that the teachers we follow and the doctrines they teach

---

adhere to the gospel of Jesus Christ, not distorting its message of grace. We are to test every teaching we receive according to the gospel as it has been revealed in the scriptures. It is interesting that we are specifically warned of false teachings received from angels, as at least two major world religions, Islam and Mormonism, trace their origins back to angelic visitations, viewing themselves as corrections and enhancements to the Christian faith.

The false gospel that was threatening the Galatian church was a form of ethno-centric legalism. As we saw in the letter to the Romans, the Jewish people had been chosen by God to steward the promise of the Messiah until He came. Many of the first Christians were indeed Jews who had turned to Jesus as the Messiah. Yet as missionaries like Paul took the gospel expanded to Gentile regions, some Jewish Christians felt that their way of life was being threatened because the Gentile Christians did not appreciate the Jewish roots of their faith and refused to follow the Jewish religious laws. Some of them began spreading word among the churches that Gentiles could be saved only if they agreed to follow all of the Jewish laws–in essence, they must become like Jews to be saved. For men, this meant being circumcised, the distinguishing mark of inclusion in the Israelite community. One can easily see why this would have been troubling for the Gentiles.

This sort of false-teaching still rears its head today when churches send out a message that one must conform to their preferred practices in order to be Christians. Legalism adds to the Gospel, insisting that one must follow Jesus AND whatever cultural practice or personal convictions we promote. The message of the book of Galatians is that Jesus alone saves and that we can worship Him while freely retaining our cultural identity.

> - *Why is it important to guard against false teaching? How can we evaluate whether a teaching we encounter is in line with the gospel of Christ?*
> - *Why is legalism so contrary to the Gospel of Christ?*
> - *Have you ever encountered "Jesus AND..." teaching in the church? How did that make you feel about yourself or your own culture? How did that personally affect your image of Christ and his followers?*
> - *What would a church look like that refused to allow "Jesus AND..." teaching to be a part of their practice?*

[11] Dear brothers and sisters, I want you to understand that the gospel message I preach is not based on mere human reasoning. [12] I received my message from no human source, and no one taught me. Instead, I received it by direct revelation from Jesus Christ.

[13] You know what I was like when I followed the Jewish religion—how I violently persecuted God's church. I did my best to destroy it. [14] I was far ahead of my fellow Jews in my zeal for the traditions of my ancestors.

[15] But even before I was born, God chose me and called me by his marvelous grace. Then it pleased him [16] to reveal his Son to me so that I would proclaim the Good News about Jesus to the Gentiles.

When this happened, I did not rush out to consult with any human being. [17] Nor did I go up to Jerusalem to consult with those who were apostles before I was. Instead, I went away into Arabia, and later I returned to the city of Damascus.

[18] Then three years later I went to Jerusalem to get to know Peter, and I stayed with him for fifteen days. [19] The only other apostle I met at that time was James, the Lord's brother. [20] I declare before God that what I am writing to you is not a lie.

[21] After that visit I went north into the provinces of Syria and Cilicia. [22] And still the churches in Christ that are in Judea didn't know me personally. [23] All they knew was that people were saying, "The one

who used to persecute us is now preaching the very faith he tried to destroy!" ²⁴ And they praised God because of me.

2 Then fourteen years later I went back to Jerusalem again, this time with Barnabas; and Titus came along, too. ² I went there because God revealed to me that I should go. While I was there I met privately with those considered to be leaders of the church and shared with them the message I had been preaching to the Gentiles. I wanted to make sure that we were in agreement, for fear that all my efforts had been wasted and I was running the race for nothing. ³ And they supported me and did not even demand that my companion Titus be circumcised, though he was a Gentile.

⁴ Even that question came up only because of some so-called believers there—false ones, really—who were secretly brought in. They sneaked in to spy on us and take away the freedom we have in Christ Jesus. They wanted to enslave us and force us to follow their Jewish regulations. ⁵ But we refused to give in to them for a single moment. We wanted to preserve the truth of the gospel message for you.

⁶ And the leaders of the church had nothing to add to what I was preaching. (By the way, their reputation as great leaders made no difference to me, for God has no favorites.) ⁷ Instead, they saw that God had given me the responsibility of preaching the gospel to the Gentiles, just as he had given Peter the responsibility of preaching to the Jews. ⁸ For the same God who worked through Peter as the apostle to the Jews also worked through me as the apostle to the Gentiles.

⁹ In fact, James, Peter, and John, who were known as pillars of the church, recognized the gift God had given me, and they accepted Barnabas and me as their co-workers. They encouraged us to keep preaching to the Gentiles, while they continued their work with the Jews. ¹⁰ Their only suggestion was that we keep on helping the poor, which I have always been eager to do.

¹¹ But when Peter came to Antioch, I had to oppose him to his face, for what he did was very wrong. ¹² When he first arrived, he ate

with the Gentile believers, who were not circumcised. But afterward, when some friends of James came, Peter wouldn't eat with the Gentiles anymore. He was afraid of criticism from these people who insisted on the necessity of circumcision. [13] As a result, other Jewish believers followed Peter's hypocrisy, and even Barnabas was led astray by their hypocrisy.

[14] When I saw that they were not following the truth of the gospel message, I said to Peter in front of all the others, "Since you, a Jew by birth, have discarded the Jewish laws and are living like a Gentile, why are you now trying to make these Gentiles follow the Jewish traditions?

☞ Guidepost 20
Christian Freedom is Secured for All in Christ Alone

[15] We ourselves are Jews by birth and not Gentile sinners; [16] yet we know that a person is not justified by works of the law but through faith in Jesus Christ, so we also have believed in Christ Jesus, in order to be justified by faith in Christ and not by works of the law, because by works of the law no one will be justified.

[17] But if, in our endeavor to be justified in Christ, we too were found to be sinners, is Christ then a servant of sin? Certainly not! [18] For if I rebuild what I tore down, I prove myself to be a transgressor. [19] For through the law I died to the law, so that I might live to God. [20] I have been crucified with Christ. It is no longer I who live, but Christ who lives in me. And the life I now live in the flesh I live by faith in the Son of God, who loved me and gave himself for me. [21] I do not nullify the grace of God, for if righteousness were through the law, then Christ died for no purpose.

3 O foolish Galatians! Who has bewitched you? It was before your eyes that Jesus Christ was publicly portrayed as crucified. ² Let me ask you only this: Did you receive the Spirit by works of the law or by hearing with faith? ³ Are you so foolish? Having begun by the Spirit, are you now being perfected by the flesh? ⁴ Did you suffer so many things in vain–if indeed it was in vain? ⁵ Does he who supplies the Spirit to you and works miracles among you do so by works of the law, or by hearing with faith⁶–just as Abraham "believed God, and it was counted to him as righteousness"?

⁷ Know then that it is those of faith who are the sons of Abraham. ⁸ And the Scripture, foreseeing that God would justify the Gentiles by faith, preached the gospel beforehand to Abraham, saying, "In you shall all the nations be blessed." ⁹ So then, those who are of faith are blessed along with Abraham, the man of faith.

☞ Discussion 20
What does this guidepost teach about freedom in Christ?

Legalism deceives us into dividing up the world into good people and bad people. Those who follow our rules and look like us are "good" while the rest are "sinners". Paul sarcastically uses the words of the legalists against them. In calling Gentiles "sinners," they are denying the gospel that teaches that all have sinned and fallen short of the glory of God. In adding to the gospel, they are nullifying God's grace, for it is no longer Jesus who saves, but what we do in addition to faith in Jesus that saves. By adding rules to the gospel for others, we end up condemning ourselves, because we have proved ourselves thoroughly incapable of following the very rules we ask others to follow.

Salvation is secured by Christ alone by faith. The Galatians should have known this because they received the Holy Spirit when they believed in Christ, long before the legalists ever showed up to teach them their rules. Moreover, the false teachers were mishandling scripture. Instead of condemning the Gentiles as "sinners", God declared to Abraham in the Jewish Scriptures that people from every nation would find salvation as they turned to Christ by faith. No one is to be excluded from God's kingdom on the basis of his or her nationality, ethnicity, social class, or gender.

- *How do we distort the gospel when we divide up the world into "good" and "bad" people?*
- *Notice how Paul counters the gospel of the legalists by pointing out how they were not acting in accord with the scriptures. What would it take for you to be able to counter false teaching in this way?*
- *What does it mean for Christianity to allow for differing cultural expressions of the faith? Does this freedom undermine the unity of the church?*

10 But those who depend on the law to make them right with God are under his curse, for the Scriptures say, "Cursed is everyone who does not observe and obey all the commands that are written in God's Book of the Law." 11 So it is clear that no one can be made right with God by trying to keep the law. For the Scriptures say, "It is through faith that a righteous person has life." 12 This way of faith is very different from the way of law, which says, "It is through obeying the law that a person has life."

13 But Christ has rescued us from the curse pronounced by the law. When he was hung on the cross, he took upon himself the curse for our wrongdoing. For it is written in the Scriptures, "Cursed is everyone who is hung on a tree." 14 Through Christ Jesus, God has blessed the Gentiles with the same blessing he promised to Abraham,

so that we who are believers might receive the promised Holy Spirit through faith.

¹⁵ Dear brothers and sisters, here's an example from everyday life. Just as no one can set aside or amend an irrevocable agreement, so it is in this case. ¹⁶ God gave the promises to Abraham and his child. And notice that the Scripture doesn't say "to his children," as if it meant many descendants. Rather, it says "to his child"—and that, of course, means Christ. ¹⁷ This is what I am trying to say: The agreement God made with Abraham could not be canceled 430 years later when God gave the law to Moses. God would be breaking his promise. ¹⁸ For if the inheritance could be received by keeping the law, then it would not be the result of accepting God's promise. But God graciously gave it to Abraham as a promise.

¹⁹ Why, then, was the law given? It was given alongside the promise to show people their sins. But the law was designed to last only until the coming of the child who was promised. God gave his law through angels to Moses, who was the mediator between God and the people. ²⁰ Now a mediator is helpful if more than one party must reach an agreement. But God, who is one, did not use a mediator when he gave his promise to Abraham.

²¹ Is there a conflict, then, between God's law and God's promises? Absolutely not! If the law could give us new life, we could be made right with God by obeying it. ²² But the Scriptures declare that we are all prisoners of sin, so we receive God's promise of freedom only by believing in Jesus Christ.

²³ Before the way of faith in Christ was available to us, we were placed under guard by the law. We were kept in protective custody, so to speak, until the way of faith was revealed.

²⁴ Let me put it another way. The law was our guardian until Christ came; it protected us until we could be made right with God through faith. ²⁵ And now that the way of faith has come, we no longer need the law as our guardian.

²⁶ For you are all children of God through faith in Christ Jesus. ²⁷ And all who have been united with Christ in baptism have put on

Christ, like putting on new clothes. ²⁸ There is no longer Jew or Gentile, slave or free, male and female. For you are all one in Christ Jesus. ²⁹ And now that you belong to Christ, you are the true children of Abraham. You are his heirs, and God's promise to Abraham belongs to you.

4 Think of it this way. If a father dies and leaves an inheritance for his young children, those children are not much better off than slaves until they grow up, even though they actually own everything their father had. ² They have to obey their guardians until they reach whatever age their father set. ³ And that's the way it was with us before Christ came. We were like children; we were slaves to the basic spiritual principles of this world.

⁴ But when the right time came, God sent his Son, born of a woman, subject to the law. ⁵ God sent him to buy freedom for us who were slaves to the law, so that he could adopt us as his very own children. ⁶ And because we are his children, God has sent the Spirit of his Son into our hearts, prompting us to call out, "Abba, Father." ⁷ Now you are no longer a slave but God's own child. And since you are his child, God has made you his heir.

⁸ Before you Gentiles knew God, you were slaves to so-called gods that do not even exist. ⁹ So now that you know God (or should I say, now that God knows you), why do you want to go back again and become slaves once more to the weak and useless spiritual principles of this world? ¹⁰ You are trying to earn favor with God by observing certain days or months or seasons or years. ¹¹ I fear for you. Perhaps all my hard work with you was for nothing. ¹² Dear brothers and sisters, I plead with you to live as I do in freedom from these things, for I have become like you Gentiles—free from those laws.

You did not mistreat me when I first preached to you. ¹³ Surely you remember that I was sick when I first brought you the Good News. ¹⁴ But even though my condition tempted you to reject me, you did not despise me or turn me away. No, you took me in and cared for me as though I were an angel from God or even Christ Jesus himself. [15] Where is that joyful and grateful spirit you felt then? I am sure you would have taken out your own eyes and given them to me if it had been possible. [16] Have I now become your enemy because I am telling you the truth?

[17] Those false teachers are so eager to win your favor, but their intentions are not good. They are trying to shut you off from me so that you will pay attention only to them. [18] If someone is eager to do good things for you, that's all right; but let them do it all the time, not just when I'm with you.

[19] Oh, my dear children! I feel as if I'm going through labor pains for you again, and they will continue until Christ is fully developed in your lives. [20] I wish I were with you right now so I could change my tone. But at this distance I don't know how else to help you.

[21] Tell me, you who want to live under the law, do you know what the law actually says? [22] The Scriptures say that Abraham had two sons, one from his slave wife and one from his freeborn wife. [23] The son of the slave wife was born in a human attempt to bring about the fulfillment of God's promise. But the son of the freeborn wife was born as God's own fulfillment of his promise.

[24] These two women serve as an illustration of God's two covenants. The first woman, Hagar, represents Mount Sinai where people received the law that enslaved them. [25] And now Jerusalem is just like Mount Sinai in Arabia, because she and her children live in slavery to the law. [26] But the other woman, Sarah, represents the heavenly Jerusalem. She is the free woman, and she is our mother. [27] As Isaiah said, "Rejoice, O childless woman, you who have never given birth! Break into a joyful shout, you who have never been in labor! For the desolate woman now has more children than the woman who lives with her husband!"

[28] And you, dear brothers and sisters, are children of the promise, just like Isaac. [29] But you are now being persecuted by those who want you to keep the law, just as Ishmael, the child born by human effort, persecuted Isaac, the child born by the power of the Spirit.

³⁰ But what do the Scriptures say about that? "Get rid of the slave and her son, for the son of the slave woman will not share the inheritance with the free woman's son." ³¹ So, dear brothers and sisters, we are not children of the slave woman; we are children of the free woman.

5 So Christ has truly set us free. Now make sure that you stay free, and don't get tied up again in slavery to the law.

² Listen! I, Paul, tell you this: If you are counting on circumcision to make you right with God, then Christ will be of no benefit to you. ³ I'll say it again. If you are trying to find favor with God by being circumcised, you must obey every regulation in the whole law of Moses. ⁴ For if you are trying to make yourselves right with God by keeping the law, you have been cut off from Christ! You have fallen away from God's grace.

⁵ But we who live by the Spirit eagerly wait to receive by faith the righteousness God has promised to us. ⁶ For when we place our faith in Christ Jesus, there is no benefit in being circumcised or being uncircumcised. What is important is faith expressing itself in love.

⁷ You were running the race so well. Who has held you back from following the truth? ⁸ It certainly isn't God, for he is the one who called you to freedom. ⁹ This false teaching is like a little yeast that spreads through the whole batch of dough! ¹⁰ I am trusting the Lord to keep you from believing false teachings. God will judge that person, whoever he is, who has been confusing you.

¹¹ Dear brothers and sisters, if I were still preaching that you must be circumcised—as some say I do—why am I still being persecuted? If I were no longer preaching salvation through the cross of Christ, no one would be offended. ¹² I just wish that those troublemakers who want to mutilate you by circumcision would mutilate themselves.

☩ Guidepost 21
Christian Freedom Produces Love as We Walk in the Spirit

¹³ For you have been called to live in freedom, my brothers and sisters. But don't use your freedom to satisfy your sinful nature. Instead, use your freedom to serve one another in love. ¹⁴ For the whole law can be summed up in this one command: "Love your neighbor as yourself." ¹⁵ But if you are always biting and devouring one another, watch out! Beware of destroying one another.

¹⁶ So I say, let the Holy Spirit guide your lives. Then you won't be doing what your sinful nature craves. ¹⁷ The sinful nature wants to do evil, which is just the opposite of what the Spirit wants. And the Spirit gives us desires that are the opposite of what the sinful nature desires. These two forces are constantly fighting each other, so you are not free to carry out your good intentions. ¹⁸ But when you are directed by the Spirit, you are not under obligation to the law of Moses.

¹⁹ When you follow the desires of your sinful nature, the results are very clear: sexual immorality, impurity, lustful pleasures, ²⁰idolatry, sorcery, hostility, quarreling, jealousy, outbursts of anger, selfish ambition, dissension, division, ²¹ envy, drunkenness, wild parties, and other sins like these. Let me tell you again, as I have before, that anyone living that sort of life will not inherit the Kingdom of God.

²² But the Holy Spirit produces this kind of fruit in our lives: love, joy, peace, patience, kindness, goodness, faithfulness, ²³ gentleness, and self-control. There is no law against these things!

²⁴ Those who belong to Christ Jesus have nailed the passions and desires of their sinful nature to his cross and crucified them there. ²⁵ Since we are living by the Spirit, let us follow the Spirit's leading in every part of our lives. ²⁶ Let us not become conceited, or provoke one another, or be jealous of one another.

✝ Discussion 21
What does this guidepost teach about freedom in Christ?

The freedom we are called to in the gospel provides us with an opportunity to love others. Since we no longer care to place others in categories of "good" or "bad", we are free to love all people as our neighbors. Again, the power to love in this way is not something we possess in ourselves, but is a natural result of living life in close concert with the Spirit. We have all seen the mess we make when we selfishly live out of our own desires. Yet when the Spirit controls our lives, He produces fruit of love in us which goes beyond legalistic righteousness.

How do we live in the Spirit? Each book we have studied so far has given us a part of the answer:

- **Abiding:** The Book of John taught us the power for living in the Spirit. In Jesus' illustration of the vine and the branches, we learn that the secret of walking in the spirit is abiding in Christ. This is the habit of praise and worship: the daily enjoyment of God and his promises so that we come to treasure Him more than anything else.

- **Renewing:** Romans taught us the path for living in the Spirit. In Romans 12:2, we are directed to be transformed by the renewing of our mind. This is the habit of study. Here is where we feed the Spirit within us with the Spirit's food, the Word of God. We meditate upon it, learn its principles, learn how to rightly interpret it, and develop personal convictions out of it, so that we begin to see the world through God's eyes.

- **Walking:** Galatians encourages us in the practice of living in the Spirit. We are told to keep in step with the Spirit. This is the habit of obedience. This is not legalistic obedience, but

---

Spirit-led obedience that naturally overflows from the first two principles. I abide in the Spirit so I know God's heart and am filled with his power. I renew my mind in the word so I know God's truth. Now I set out to live a spirit-filled life in a spirit-led manner. In doing so, I will not fulfill the lusts of the flesh.

- *How does the work of the Spirit in believers produce what mere external legalistic obedience cannot?*
- *How is freedom connected to love? Can one truly love if the love is produced by coercion?*
- *What are some practical ways that you will seek to develop the disciplines of worship, study and obedience?*
- *How can you approach these disciplines in a way that does not lead to legalism?*

6 Dear brothers and sisters, if another believer is overcome by some sin, you who are godly should gently and humbly help that person back onto the right path. And be careful not to fall into the same temptation yourself. ² Share each other's burdens, and in this way obey the law of Christ. ³ If you think you are too important to help someone, you are only fooling yourself. You are not that important.

⁴ Pay careful attention to your own work, for then you will get the satisfaction of a job well done, and you won't need to compare yourself to anyone else. ⁵ For we are each responsible for our own conduct.

⁶ Those who are taught the word of God should provide for their teachers, sharing all good things with them.

⁷ Don't be misled—you cannot mock the justice of God. You will always harvest what you plant. ⁸ Those who live only to satisfy their own sinful nature will harvest decay and death from that sinful nature. But those who live to please the Spirit will harvest everlasting life from the Spirit.⁹ So let's not get tired of doing what is good. At just

the right time we will reap a harvest of blessing if we don't give up. [10] Therefore, whenever we have the opportunity, we should do good to everyone—especially to those in the family of faith.

[11] NOTICE WHAT LARGE LETTERS I USE AS I WRITE THESE CLOSING WORDS IN MY OWN HANDWRITING.

[12] Those who are trying to force you to be circumcised want to look good to others. They don't want to be persecuted for teaching that the cross of Christ alone can save. [13] And even those who advocate circumcision don't keep the whole law themselves. They only want you to be circumcised so they can boast about it and claim you as their disciples.

[14] As for me, may I never boast about anything except the cross of our Lord Jesus Christ. Because of that cross, my interest in this world has been crucified, and the world's interest in me has also died. [15] It doesn't matter whether we have been circumcised or not. What counts is whether we have been transformed into a new creation. [16] May God's peace and mercy be upon all who live by this principle; they are the new people of God.

[17] From now on, don't let anyone trouble me with these things. For I bear on my body the scars that show I belong to Jesus.

[18] Dear brothers and sisters, may the grace of our Lord Jesus Christ be with your spirit. Amen.

Prayer:
The Psalms

The best part of the good news of the gospel is that Jesus brings believers into a relationship with the Father. The Holy Spirit inside of us is the Spirit of sonship, prompting our hearts to desire an intimate relationship with God. God has initiated a relationship with us by adopting us into His family. He continues to seek an intimate relationship with us by communicating with us through His Word and by His Spirit. We respond to God and develop intimacy in our relationship with Him through prayer.

Open your time with God by personally addressing Him in your own prayer. Always remember that you're not just praying words off of a page, but you are building a relationship with the God of the universe.

The Book of Psalms was written to guide us in learning to pray. By praying the Psalms, we learn how to express ourselves before God through any circumstance or state of our heart: through trial, doubt, pain, loneliness, joy, betrayal, wonder, depression, longing, etc. As you begin your relationship with God through Jesus Christ, develop the habit of praying a Psalm every day.

Read each line of the Psalm out loud slowly, trying to understand each phrase. If you find yourself skimming or your mind becomes distracted, go back to where you got distracted and read it again.

Sometimes a verse or phrase will stick out to you, underline it and memorize it by praying it to the Lord. The Spirit of God will speak through His word to you by drawing you to particular verses. When this happens, these are the verses and psalms you want to memorize.

"Own" the Psalm: If there is a particular Psalm that God uses in your life, do everything you can to make it your own. Memorize it. Pray it. Make it into a song. Print it out and hang it on your wall. Share it with others. Recite it to your spouse and your kids.

Here is an example of praying with Psalm 23 - The Psalm of David:

The Lord is my shepherd; I shall not want. He makes me lie down in green pastures.
He leads me beside still waters. He restores my soul.

Then in your words:

Lord, you are my shepherd. You provide for all of my needs – even those I know nothing about! I need your guidance today. I am facing so much stress at work and I don't know what to do. Help me to rest in You today. I am so anxious. Restore me, God. Restore my peace. Restore my faith.

He leads me in paths of righteousness for his name's sake.

Lead me, Lord. For Your name's sake. Not for my name. For Yours. Take my eyes off of me and my worries. Help me to live for Your name, no matter what I face at work today.

Or search for Jesus in the Psalm: As you pray and meditate on each Psalm, think of how the Psalm was fulfilled in the life of Jesus. Use this to draw you into worship of Him.

**The Lord is my shepherd; I shall not want. He makes me
lie down in green pastures.**
He leads me beside still waters. He restores my soul.
*Jesus, <u>You</u> are my shepherd. You are the good shepherd. You hear my voice
and protect me from evil. I praise You because You care for Your sheep.
You care for me. You said that You lay down Your own life for Your sheep,
and You did!*

To select a Psalm to pray, you can go chronologically or pick
selected Psalms. It may be helpful to go through the Psalms
chronologically at first until you build up a familiarity with them. The
above psalm was selected for this guide as it is well-loved by many
people, especially those facing difficult times.

When tired or upset - Psalm 5
When discouraged - Psalms 23, 42
When alone or disillusioned by a friend - Psalm 40
When filled with great happiness - Psalms 97,99,100
When grateful for the gifts of God - Psalm 135
When in need of refuge - Psalms 46, 91
When life needs a spiritual boost - Psalm 27
When worried - Psalm 34
When anguished in life - Psalms 31, 34
When needing confidence or courage - Psalms 27, 31, 56, 62
When in need of health - Psalms 6, 27, 39, 41
When in need of help - Psalms 121, 130, 146
When struggling with sin - Psalm 51
When doubting your faith - Psalm 73

What Now?

Congratulations on completing Explore! I hope that through this study you have gained a firm understanding of who Jesus is, why He came, and the basic message of the Christian faith. It is my prayer that you have come to a place where you are ready to trust Christ as your Lord and Savior and follow Him as His disciple by the leading of the Holy Spirit. You might be wondering what you should do now. Here are some possible next steps to take:

- Believe in Jesus Christ. If you have not yet done so, Appendix 1 will lead you though how you can place your faith in Christ.

- If you are not yet connected to a local church, seek one out. The Christian life was not meant to be lived in solitude. No church is perfect, but seek out one that teaches the Bible and is friendly. Take initiative in building relationships with people in the church.

- If you have come to faith in Christ, talk to a pastor or church leader about being baptized. Passing through the water symbolically marks the death of our old way of life, cleansing from our sins, and our initiation into the life of Christ. It is not the act of baptism that saves us, but the spiritual reality of our union with Christ by faith alone. Water baptism is a powerful, public testimony that a person has truly come to faith in Christ and wishes to follow Christ as his disciple. It should be done as soon as possible after it is evident that a person possesses genuine faith and has been given new life in Christ.

- Continue to study the Bible with regular reading and also with guided study.

- Guide someone else. Take a friend through this study so that they can begin exploring who Jesus is as well. Plus, teaching it will give you a deeper understanding.

Appendix 1: How to Begin a Relationship with Christ

"If you confess with your mouth that Jesus is Lord and believe in your heart that God raised him from the dead, you will be saved. For with the heart one believes and is justified, and with the mouth one confesses and is saved. For the Scripture says, "Everyone who believes in him will not be put to shame." For there is no distinction between Jew and Greek; for the same Lord is Lord of all, bestowing his riches on all who call on him. For "everyone who calls on the name of the Lord will be saved." (Romans 10:9–13)

The Bible teaches that anyone can come to God who is willing to put their hope in Jesus Christ. No external work can save us; faith is an inward orientation of the heart toward Jesus Christ. Yet our internal change of heart is expressed outwardly.

For many people, their first outward expression of faith in Christ is expressed to God through prayer. The Bible does not give us a formula to pray this expression of faith, for it is not the words of the prayer that save us, but many people pray a prayer that simply agrees with God about what He has revealed to us in the Gospel. Perhaps the most basic prayer takes the form of "I can't, You can, Please do".

I Can't: *God, I recognize that sin has separated me from you. I understand that I can do nothing to earn my salvation or your love.*

You Can: *Yet I now believe that you lovingly sent your Son, Jesus, into the world to save me. He lived the life that I couldn't live, died in my place to suffer the penalty my sins deserved and then rose from the dead. Because of what Jesus has done for me, you are able to both punish sin and be merciful to me.*

Please Do: *Though I do not deserve your love and mercy, please forgive me, come into my life, and save me. From this day forward, I will place my trust in Jesus. Amen.*

If you have sincerely come to Christ as your Lord and Savior, congratulations! You have been forgiven of your sins and adopted into God's family. The Holy Spirit will begin to transform your life from the inside out. To help you grow and receive further benefits from your life with Jesus, please tell someone immediately of your decision to follow Him so they can encourage and assist you along the path.

Appendix 2: How to Use this Book to Guide Others

I am so excited that you are would like to guide others as they explore what the Bible has to say about who Jesus is and how we can know God through Him.

STEP 1: Find Explorers

The first step to becoming a Guide is to find Explorers willing to be guided in the Christian Faith. The good news is that people are generally open to reading the Bible together with a friend, if it is done in a non-threatening manner.

Finding Explorers starts with asking everyone around you a very simple question: "Would you be willing to meet together with me once in a while to read a portion of the Bible and explore what it says about God?"

If they ask for details, say, "I suggest that we read through the Gospel of John, because it gives the clearest picture of the Bible's claims about Jesus. If we met once a week, it would take a couple of months.

Do not get discouraged if many say, "No." You need only one person to say, "Yes," to become a Guide.

STEP 2: Prepare Explorers

The second step to becoming a Guide is to prepare your Explorers for meeting together.

First, agree to meet with your Explorers at a time and place that is convenient to you. Do all you can to ensure that the place is comfortable and familiar to them. Be hospitable and generous, offering to buy them coffee or drinks if it is appropriate. Look for a place that is not too loud and affords a little privacy so that you can have good conversation.

Explain that there is an book that was created to read and explore the Bible together. Show them your book and explain that contains three books of the Bible with some important passages highlighted for you to discuss. Give them their own copy of the book.

STEP 3: Prepare Yourself

The third step to becoming a Guide is to prepare yourself for meeting together

First, pray for yourself and for your Explorers. Pray that God would give you wisdom and insight to guide the conversation. Pray that God would give your Explorers open hearts to receive the Word. Second, briefly familiarize yourself with the passage of scripture and the study guide.

STEP 4: Meet Together

When you meet together, be friendly and open. Ask them about their lives; about what they are grateful for and what challenges they are currently facing.

Honor their time. If they have agreed to meet for a half hour, then make sure you finish within that half-hour. If the study is not complete when your agreed upon time is over, ask them if they'd like to continue or wrap up.

If they ask you a difficult question, do not be afraid to say, "I don't know." Many questions that they have at the beginning may be answered later in the study. Do not become defensive or argumentative. Trust the process and the sufficiency of God's Word to answer their questions

If you are meeting with a non-Christian, ask if they would be comfortable with you praying for them as you close the study. If they say, "No," honor that. If they are ok with you praying for them, keep your prayer simple, generous, and humble. Bless them and ask God to reveal Himself to them through the study of His Word.

When your meeting is finished, ask them to read up until the next guidepost before your next meeting. Invite them to write down any questions, comments or insights that they have so that you can review them at the beginning of your next meeting.

STEP 5: Follow Up Care

Being a Guide is more than just leading someone through a Bible Study. It is about being a spiritual friend and mentor to those you are guiding. Pray for them through the week. Contact them regularly to ask about their lives. Meet practical needs in their life, thus demonstrating Christ's love to them

Explore is designed to start the process of exploring the faith outside of the local church, but it is not to be understood as existing apart from the local church. As Explorers come to faith, invite them to join you in the life of your local church.

There may come a time when you have to pass-off your Explorers to a different mentor. Perhaps you move or become sick. In that case, work with your Explorers to find an appropriate guide for them.

Also, it may be that you begin the *Explore* process with an Explorer of the opposite sex. This is appropriate for the early stages of the process. However, if your Explorer continues on in the faith, it generally is better to introduce them to someone of their own sex who can continue to guide them in the faith.

Congratulations! You are now ready to be a Guide to new Explorers!

We suggest that you set a goal of guiding at least three Explorers at all times. If any drop out of the process, look for non-Christians and those outside of the church to start again at step #1.

www.ingramcontent.com/pod-product-compliance
Lightning Source LLC
Chambersburg PA
CBHW060939040426
42445CB00011B/929